FOUR SHERLOCK HOLMES PLAYS

Four
Sherlock Holmes Plays

ONE-ACT PLAYS BY

MICHAEL & MOLLIE HARDWICK

FROM STORIES BY

SIR ARTHUR CONAN DOYLE

JOHN MURRAY

Fifty Albemarle Street London

These plays are fully protected by copy-
right and no performance may be given
without a licence from

The League of Dramatists
84, Drayton Gardens,
London, S.W.10

from whose Secretary all information about
fees can be obtained.

© MICHAEL & MOLLIE HARDWICK 1964
First published 1964
Second impression 1966

Printed in Great Britain by
Cox & Wyman Ltd, London
Fakenham and Reading

FOREWORD

There are certain authors – Dickens is a shining example – whose books transform naturally into plays. Most of them wrote for the stage at some time or other, and today they would be busy with the mass media of radio, television and film. Sir Arthur Conan Doyle was such a writer. (One can imagine him groaning under the burden of a popular television series, impatient to escape to his next fourteenth-century chronicle.) It is no lucky chance that the radio adaptations of the Sherlock Holmes stories have been broadcast so widely at home and abroad: the original works from which the radio plays were made are perfect for such adaptation; we, as their adapters, merely function, like Watson, as 'conductors of light'.

Curiously, few of the Holmes and Watson adventures have been made into plays for the stage: and then often in the form of composite plots, made up of elements from several of the original stories. Yet each story translates itself quite naturally into stage form, without mechanical difficulties, with compactness of setting and movement, retaining those qualities of compulsion, drama, humour and wisdom which have made them the most famous detective story classics.

At Christmas, 1963, while the volume was in preparation, we were given the invaluable opportunity of trying out one of these plays. *The Blue Carbuncle*, with its Christmas theme, seemed to us an admirable novelty to offer to schools for end-of-term production at that time of the year; and we were grateful when Mr. C. I. R. Burton, the progressive headmaster of Betteshanger Preparatory School, in Kent, undertook not only to present the play, but to produce it himself.

The cast of this 'world premiere' included no boy over the age of thirteen, and several much younger. Only three or four weeks were available for preparations, following immediately upon the tension of Common Entrance examinations, while several of the cast were also choristers, with a heavy list of Christmas engagements. Despite all this, the production was a resounding success.

Our radio adaptations, from which these stage versions derive, owe much to the British Broadcasting Corporation's considerable resources and to the services of some of the world's best radio actors, producers and technicians. The Betteshanger School's production showed that these plays can also thrive upon the proverbial shoe-string: without a proscenium stage, without scenery, without hired period costume, with a handful of borrowed properties and with the simplest of lighting, rigged and operated by a boy of thirteen who also acted. It proved that a detective adventure can be as suitable for a cast (and audience) of children as it is for adult professionals or amateurs, and that Holmes and Watson are as much in their element on the stage as in any other medium.

We sincerely hope that, whether acting in these plays or seeing them as one of the audience, reading them in the classroom or by the fireside at home, you will find that they retain the qualities which have immortalized Sir Arthur Conan Doyle's Sherlock Holmes stories.

MICHAEL & MOLLIE HARDWICK

CONTENTS

The authors wish to express their gratitude to the Trustees of the Estate of the late Sir Arthur Conan Doyle.

NOTES FOR PRODUCERS

The following texts have been kept as unencumbered by stage directions and demands for precise settings and properties as possible. The aim has been to include only information which is essential for the dual purpose of reading the plays or for mounting the simplest production. Well-endowed, or especially resourceful, producers may elaborate as they wish; for others all the essentials are implicit in the dialogue.

Except in the case of *The Speckled Band*, scenery can, if necessary, be dispensed with; the plays could be presented on an open stage with a minimum of properties and the merest suggestion of costume.

The parlour of 221B Baker Street is shown in all its wealth of detail in the frontispiece to this volume: that immortal clutter can be reduced, without any loss of effect, to a couple of chairs, a lamp, and a table with decanter and glasses. For the Betteshanger School production of *The Blue Carbuncle* Holmes was provided with the additional luxury of a desk, successively converted into the bar of the Alpha Inn and Breckinridge's poultry stall. These conversions and all other changes of properties were carried out in full view of the audience, who appeared to enjoy them hugely, and the practice can be confidently recommended.

There are no difficulties: merely a challenge or two. The substitution of the live Holmes for his dummy representation in *The Mazarin Stone* calls for some careful staging and rehearsal. In *The Speckled Band* the appearance of the snake implies thought, ingenuity and skill; but the result ought to be electrifying. A three-act version of *The Speckled Band* – much intermixed with ingredients and characters from other

stories – was presented with great success more than half a century ago and used, at first, a real snake. In very little time the snake had to be replaced by an ingeniously jointed model worked by threads, and we recommend our readers to take the lesson as learnt!

May we make one plea? That any temptation towards burlesque should sternly be resisted. Cackling villains and the clutching of brows are out! The staid Victorians were not above showing their feelings, but not in terms of the exaggerated conventions of melodrama. Strange though the Sherlock Holmes stories may seem nowadays, their intrinsic magic makes them credible if it is allowed to do so – and they have been taken seriously enough to be made required reading in the police forces of several countries.

Of the characters of Holmes and Watson surely little need be said? The sardonic, ascetic, ubiquitous Holmes springs so vividly from his every utterance that the physical attributes of the actor portraying him matter very little. Of Watson let it merely be noted that he is by no means the fool that some portrayals have made him out to be.

Two final recommendations: advertising and publicity will be found to be more effective if the words 'Sherlock Holmes and . . .' are incorporated in the title of each play: e.g. *Sherlock Holmes and The Speckled Band*. For a double-bill presentation of any of these plays the title *Studies in Sherlock* is suggested.

The comprehension and ability of the actors and auxiliaries alike – not to mention the enjoyment of the task in hand – will be immeasurably increased if they read Sir Arthur Conan Doyle's original stories as well as these versions for acting.

THE SPECKLED BAND

Characters in order of appearance :

SHERLOCK HOLMES

MRS. HUDSON: Holmes's landlady. She is middle-aged and may be Scottish. She dotes on him, but despairs of his habits.

DR. WATSON

HELEN STONER: A cultured, attractive lady of thirty-two 'in a pitiable state of agitation, her face all drawn and grey, with restless, frightened eyes, like those of some hunted animal.'

DR. GRIMESBY ROYLOTT: Helen's stepfather; a powerful, belligerent, middle-aged man of good family but unfortunate character. 'Violence of temper approaching to mania has been hereditary in the men of the family . . .'

A SNAKE

THE SPECKLED BAND

SCENE ONE

> [*The parlour of* 221B *Baker Street. A coffee-pot and its attendant accessories stand on a small table.* HOLMES, *warming his back at the fire, is talking with* MRS. HUDSON, *who stands in the parlour doorway*]

HOLMES: All right, Mrs. Hudson. I'll see the lady at once.

MRS. HUDSON: Very good, Mr. Holmes.

> [*She turns to exit and collides with* WATSON, *who is bustling in*]

WATSON: Oops!

MRS. HUDSON: I beg your pardon, sir.

WATSON: My fault entirely, Mrs. Hudson.

> [MRS. HUDSON *exits, closing the door.* WATSON, *rubbing his hands briskly together, crosses to the coffee things and pours himself a cup*]

Morning, Holmes!

HOLMES: Good morning, my dear Watson! You're just in time.

WATSON: Eh? What for?

HOLMES: We have a client.

WATSON: What – already!

HOLMES: It seems that a young lady has arrived in a considerable state of excitement.

WATSON: Aha!

HOLMES: Now, when young ladies wander about the metropolis at this hour of the morning I presume they have something very pressing to communicate. Should it prove so, I'm sure you would wish to follow the case from the outset?

WATSON: My dear fellow, I wouldn't miss it for anything! [*with a leer*] Young lady, d'ye say?

HOLMES: Watson!

[*A knock at the parlour door.* MRS. HUDSON *enters*]

MRS. HUDSON: Miss Helen Stoner, sir.

[*She steps aside to admit* HELEN, *then goes out, closing the door.* HOLMES *advances with hand outstretched, as* WATSON *hastily lays aside his coffee-cup with interest*]

HOLMES: Good morning, madam. My name is Sherlock Holmes.

HELEN [*her voice betrays tension*]: Good morning, Mr. Holmes.

HOLMES: And this is my intimate friend and colleague, Dr. Watson.

WATSON: How d'ye do, ma'am?

HELEN: How do you do, Doctor?

WATSON: You're cold, ma'am! Let me pour you a cup of coffee.

[*He starts off towards the coffee, but* HELEN *checks him*]

HELEN: No coffee, thank you. It's not . . . the cold.

WATSON: But you're shivering!

HELEN: From fear, Dr. Watson. From terror!

[HOLMES *moves to her and steers her to a fireside chair. He takes the one opposite her,* WATSON *assuming his position at* HOLMES'S *elbow*]

HOLMES: Don't be afraid, Miss Stoner. We shall soon set matters right.

HELEN: If only you can!

HOLMES: You have come in by train this morning, I see.

HELEN [*surprised*]: How do you know that?

HOLMES [*pointing*]: There is the second half of a return ticket tucked into your left glove.

HELEN: Oh!

HOLMES: I see you also had a good ride in a dog-cart, along heavy roads, on your way to the station.

HELEN: Yes! But I don't see how you can possibly . . .

HOLMES [*interrupting her*]: There is no mystery, my dear madam. The left arm of your jacket is spattered with mud in no less than seven places. The marks are perfectly fresh. Only a dog-cart throws up mud in that way.

HELEN [*urgently*]: Mr. Holmes, I have no one to turn to! No one!

HOLMES: Calm yourself, dear lady.

HELEN [*sobbing*]: I can stand this strain no longer!

> [HELEN *dabs at her eyes.* WATSON *makes an instinctive move towards the brandy decanter, but* HOLMES *restrains him*]

HOLMES: Tell me what I can do for you.

HELEN [*recovering*]: Forgive me, Mr. Holmes. If . . . if you can throw a little light through the darkness which seems to surround me . . .

HOLMES: Let us hope so.

HELEN: I . . . I must tell you that I can't pay for your services at present. But in a month or two I shall be married and have control of my own income.

WATSON [*a little disappointed*]: Er, congratulations!

HOLMES: My profession is its own reward. Now kindly let us hear everything that may help us to form an opinion.

HELEN: Very well. [*She settles back, a little more relaxed*]. My mother was the young widow of Major-General Stoner.

WATSON: Bengal Artillery?

HELEN: Yes.

WATSON [*impressed*]: By Jove!

[*He catches a meaningful glance from* HOLMES]

Sorry, Holmes! Pray go on, ma'am.

HELEN: When my twin sister, Julia, and I were two my mother re-married to Dr. Grimesby Roylott, of Stoke Moran, on the western border of Surrey. About eight years ago my mother was killed in a railway accident at Crewe.

[WATSON *makes a sympathetic sound*]

HOLMES: Leaving you and your sister in the care of your stepfather.

HELEN: Exactly, Mr. Holmes. My mother had a great deal of money. She bequeathed it all to Dr. Roylott, with a provision that a certain annual sum should be allowed to my sister and me in the event of our marriage.

HOLMES: I understand. If I'm not mistaken, the Roylott family is one of the oldest Saxon families in England.

HELEN: And at one time amongst the richest, too. But the fortune was wasted in the last century by four successive heirs. The last squire dragged out his existence as an aristocratic pauper, and all my stepfather inherited was a few acres of land and a 200-year-old house.

HOLMES: When was this?

HELEN: Oh, a good many years before he married my mother. He saw that he must adapt himself to conditions, so he took a medical degree. He went out to Calcutta

and established a large practice. Unfortunately . . . [*she hesitates*].

HOLMES: Yes?

HELEN: He . . . in a fit of anger, he beat his butler to death.

WATSON: Good heavens!

HELEN: He escaped a capital sentence, but spent several years in prison.

HOLMES: And it was after his release that he married your mother?

HELEN: That is so. We all came back to England together, and my stepfather tried to establish a new practice here. But then . . . my mother was killed, and he took Julia and me to live with him in the ancestral home at Stoke Moran. It . . . it was about this time that a terrible change came over him.

HOLMES: A change? Of what kind?

HELEN: There was a series of disgraceful quarrels and brawls with anyone giving him the least offence. Two of them ended in the police court. My stepfather is a man of immense strength and absolutely uncontrollable anger. Only last week he threw the local blacksmith over a parapet into a stream.

[WATSON *whistles*]

WATSON [*apologetically*]: Er, I beg your pardon!

HELEN: He's become the terror of the village, until his only friends are the wandering gipsies. He gives them leave to camp on what remains of the estate. Oh, and he has his animals.

WATSON: He's farming now?

HELEN: Nothing like that, I'm afraid, Doctor. He has a passion for Indian animals. At this moment he has a cheetah and a baboon wandering quite freely in the grounds.

B

WATSON: Jove!

HOLMES: But your story is incomplete, Miss Stoner.

HELEN: I'm sorry. I was just going to add that, with this state of affairs, no servant would stay in the house, and so my poor sister and I had all the housework to do. You can imagine we had little pleasure in our lives.

[HOLMES *nods sympathetically*]

Poor Julia's hair had already begun to turn white at the time of her death.

[HOLMES *leans forward interestedly*]

HOLMES: Your sister is dead, then?

HELEN: She died just two years ago. She was thirty. It . . . it was just a fortnight before she should have been married.

HOLMES [*halting her with a gesture*]: Miss Stoner – pray be precise about the details from this point.

HELEN: That will be easy. Every event of that dreadful time is seared into my memory.

HOLMES: Quite so.

HELEN: As I told you, the manor house is very old. Only one wing is now inhabited. The bedrooms are on the ground floor, all in a row, opening out into the same corridor. The first is Dr. Roylott's, the second was my sister's, the third mine. Do I make myself plain?

HOLMES: Perfectly. Watson?

WATSON: Three bedrooms in a row – your stepfather's, your late sister's, and then your own. Yes, I've got it.

HELEN: The windows of all three rooms open on to the lawn. Well, on that fatal night . . .

HOLMES [*interrupting her*]: One moment, Miss Stoner. You are about to tell us of your sister's death?

HELEN: Why, yes!

HOLMES: I see. And we understand, do we not, that some

Sherlock Holmes's sitting-room at 221B Baker Street

(Reproduced by permission of St Marylebone Public Libraries Committee)

time before this event occurred, your sister had announced her intention of marrying?

HELEN: That's correct. Only a short while before, actually. She'd met her fiancé during a visit to our aunt's house at Harrow. He was a major of Marines, on half-pay.

HOLMES: Did your stepfather oppose the match?

HELEN: No.

HOLMES: Then pray continue.

HELEN: On the night in question, Julia and I were sitting in her room, talking about her wedding arrangements. Dr. Roylott was in his room next door. We could smell his cigar. Well, I rose to leave my sister at eleven o'clock, but she stopped me at the door and asked something rather strange.

WATSON: What was that?

HELEN: Whether I had ever heard anyone whistle in the dead of the night.

WATSON: Whistle?

HELEN: I told her I hadn't. Then she said that on the past three nights she had been woken by a long, low whistle. She couldn't tell where it came from, and we put it down to the gipsies in the plantation near by. Then I went off to my room, and I locked my door and went to bed.

HOLMES: You locked your door?

HELEN: I heard her key turn, too, as usual. With a cheetah and a baboon at large we had no feeling of security if our doors weren't locked.

HOLMES: I understand.

HELEN: I couldn't sleep that night. It was very wild outside, with the wind howling and the rain beating and splashing. Suddenly, amidst all the noise, I heard my sister scream. I turned my key and rushed into the corridor. Just as I did so, I seemed to hear a low whistle. I was in

time to see my sister's door swing slowly open. I was rooted to the spot. I didn't know what I expected to see come out. Then, by the light of the corridor lamp, I saw my sister emerge. She was swaying . . . her face was blanched with terror . . . her hands seemed to be groping for help . . . Oh!

> [HELEN *buries her face in her hands.* HOLMES *and* WATSON *exchange mystified glances*]

HOLMES: Take your time, ma'am.

HELEN [*recovering with a determined effort*]: I must tell you it all. I . . . ran to my sister. I threw my arms round her. But at that moment her knees seemed to give way and she fell to the ground. She . . . she writhed, as though in terrible pain. I thought she hadn't recognized me, but as I bent over her she suddenly shrieked out . . . 'Helen! It was a band! The speckled band!'

HOLMES: 'The speckled band?' Those were her exact words?

HELEN: I shall never forget them. It was the last time I heard her voice. As my stepfather came out of his room, pulling on his dressing-gown, she died in my arms. [*Faintly*] Such was the dreadful end of my beloved sister.

> [WATSON *goes to the brandy, pours her a glass and gives it to her. She sips it gratefully*]

Thank you, Doctor.

HOLMES: This whistle you say you heard – can you be sure?

HELEN: I have asked myself that sometimes.

WATSON: The wind and rain, Holmes. The old house creaking.

HELEN: I still think it was a whistle. That was what I swore to the Coroner.

HOLMES: Was your sister dressed?

HELEN: No, she was in her nightdress. We found a spent match in one of her hands, and a matchbox in the other.

HOLMES: Showing that she had struck a light and looked around when she was alarmed. That is important.

WATSON: What conclusion did the Coroner come to, Miss Stoner?

HELEN: He was unable to find any satisfactory cause of death. Her door had been locked on the inside. Her window was shut and locked. She must have been quite alone when whatever it was happened to her.

WATSON: Were there any marks of violence on her?

HELEN: None at all.

WATSON: What about poison?

HELEN: The doctors could find no traces.

HOLMES: Miss Stoner . . .

HELEN: Yes, Mr. Holmes?

HOLMES: What do *you* think this unfortunate lady died of?

HELEN: I believe she died of fear, Mr. Holmes. Of pure terror.

HOLMES: And what do you imagine frightened her?

HELEN [*shaking her head slowly*]: I don't know.

WATSON [*inspired*]: Holmes – that reference to a 'speckled band'. Well, couldn't that be to do with the gipsies who were near? A *band* of gipsies . . . or . . . or even those spotted handkerchief things they wear on their heads. Speckled bands?

HOLMES: An interesting idea, Watson. These are very deep waters. Miss Stoner, please bring your narrative up to date now.

HELEN: Very well. All that was two years ago, as I told you. Since than, my life has been lonelier and unhappier than ever. However, a dear friend whom I've known for years has asked me to marry him. We . . . we're to be married in a few weeks' time.

HOLMES: What is your stepfather's view of that?

HELEN: He's offered no opposition whatever. But a strange thing has happened . . . sufficient to terrify me.

HOLMES: Please go on.

HELEN: Two days ago some building repairs were ordered and my bedroom wall is affected. I have had to move into the room my sister occupied at the time of her death.

WATSON: Next to your stepfather's.

HELEN: Yes. I'm . . . I'm sleeping in the very bed poor Julia slept in. You can imagine my terror last night, then, when I heard that same low whistling sound.

WATSON: Great heavens!

HELEN: I sprang up and lit the lamp. But there was nothing to be seen in the room. I was too shaken to go to bed again. I got dressed, and as soon as it was daylight I slipped down to the Crown Inn and got a dog-cart to drive me to the station at Leatherhead. My object was to see you, Mr. Holmes, and to ask your advice.

HOLMES: You were wise to do so, Miss Stoner. But have you told me everything?

HELEN: Yes, I have.

HOLMES: I fancy you have not!

HELEN: Mr. Holmes!

[HOLMES *leans forward and turns back the fringe of dress at one of her wrists*]

HOLMES: If you will permit me? Thank you. You see, Watson?

[WATSON *peers*]

WATSON: Those are bruises from four fingers and a thumb!

HOLMES: Precisely. You have been cruelly used, madam.

[*He withdraws his hand*]

HELEN [*flustered*]: He . . . he is a hard man. But he *is* my step-father. He . . . doesn't know his own strength. That is all.

HOLMES: If you insist. Miss Stoner, there are a thousand details that I should like to know before we decide on a course of action. If we were to come to Stoke Moran today . . .

HELEN: Today!

HOLMES: Believe me, there isn't a moment to lose. If we came, would it be possible for us to see over these rooms without your stepfather's knowledge?

[HELEN *gets to her feet*]

HELEN: He spoke of coming to town today on some important business. He will probably be away from home all day.

HOLMES [*getting up*]: Excellent! Will your servants be discreet?

HELEN: We only have a housekeeper. She's old and foolish. I could easily get her out of the way.

HOLMES: Then we shall come – that is, if you're not averse to the trip, Watson?

WATSON: By no means.

HELEN: I should like to do one or two things, now that I'm in town. I shall be back by the twelve o'clock train, and be at Stoke Moran in time to meet you.

HOLMES: Capital!

[*He guides her towards the door*]

You're *sure* you won't stay for some breakfast?

HELEN [*hesitates*]: Well . . .

[HOLMES *whips open the door and bows*]

HOLMES: Then you may expect to see us early this afternoon. Good day, Miss Stoner.

HELEN: Good day, gentlemen.

[*She exits*]

WATSON: Good day.

[HOLMES *closes the door*]

Holmes! You invite her to breakfast, then almost push her out!

HOLMES [*seriously*] : We have some business of our own to attend to before we go down there. What do you think of it all, Watson?

WATSON [*troubled*] : Dark and sinister – that's what I think of it, Holmes.

[HOLMES *takes his pipe and tobacco from the mantelpiece, and fills and lights it during the following dialogue*]

HOLMES: Dark enough and sinister enough.

WATSON: But, Holmes – if she's correct in saying the door and window of her sister's room were locked, then the girl must have been absolutely alone when she met her death.

HOLMES: Death in a sealed room, in fact?

WATSON: Natural causes. No other explanation. [*Scratching his head*] But then, what about that whistling in the night – and that speckled band business?

HOLMES: I was hoping *you* were going to provide me with those answers, my dear Watson.

WATSON: Well, you'll have to hope again!

HOLMES [*mock dismay*] : Dear me!

WATSON: Have you any ideas?

HOLMES: We have whistles at night, a band of gipsies . . .

WATSON: Yes.

HOLMES: . . . a doctor who has a financial interest in preventing his stepdaughter's marriage.

WATSON: Ah, yes!

HOLMES: And we have a dying reference to a speckled band. Now, if we combine all these elements, I think there is good ground to believe that the mystery may be cleared up.

WATSON: Well, then – the gipsies: what did they do?

HOLMES: I can't imagine.

WATSON: Neither can I!

HOLMES: It's precisely for that reason that we're going to Stoke Moran today.

> [*A disturbance outside the parlour door, caused by* MRS. HUDSON *approaching, protesting vigorously, and* ROYLOTT *insisting on being allowed to pass*]

I want to see just how much can be explained . . . What in the name of the devil . . .?

> [*The parlour door is flung open, revealing* ROY-LOTT *in a challenging attitude*]

ROYLOTT: Which of you two is Holmes?

MRS. HUDSON [*at his elbow*]: I tried to prevent this gentleman, sir. He would insist.

HOLMES [*calmly*]: That's all right, Mrs. Hudson. Kindly close the door as you go.

MRS. HUDSON: Yes, sir.

> [MRS. HUDSON *goes, closing the door.* ROY-LOTT *advances belligerently upon* HOLMES]

ROYLOTT: You're Holmes, then?

HOLMES: That is my name, sir. But you have the advantage of me.

ROYLOTT: I am Dr. Grimesby Roylott, of Stoke Moran.

HOLMES: Indeed, Doctor! Pray take a seat. This is your professional colleague, Dr. Watson.

> [ROYLOTT *ignores both the seat and* WATSON]

ROYLOTT: I'll do nothing of the kind! My stepdaughter has

been here. I know she has! What has she been saying to you?

HOLMES: It *is* a little cold for the time of the year.

ROYLOTT: *What has she been saying?*

HOLMES: But I've heard that the crocuses promise well.

ROYLOTT [*infuriated*]: You think you can put me off, do you? But I know you, you scoundrel! You're Holmes, the meddler!

[HOLMES *chuckles*]

Holmes, the busybody!

[HOLMES *chuckles louder*]

Holmes, the Scotland Yard Jack-in-Office!

[HOLMES *laughs out loud*]

HOLMES: Your conversation is most entertaining, Dr. Roylott. When you go out, do close the door, please. [*Clasping his shoulders as though cold*] There's a decided draught.

[ROYLOTT, *beside himself with fury, waves his fists in the air.* WATSON *quietly picks up a bottle, ready to wade in.* HOLMES *stands quite still and allows the tempest to rage*]

ROYLOTT: I will go when I've had my say. [*Shaking his fist under Holmes's nose*] Don't you dare meddle with my affairs! I know the girl has been here. I warn you, Holmes, I'm a dangerous man to fall foul of!

[*He looks towards the fireplace, then strides over and picks up the poker*]

See here!

[WATSON *raises his bottle in readiness, but* ROYLOTT *grasps the poker in both hands and begins to bend it*]

I'll show you . . . how I could bend you . . . for two pins!

[*With a grunt he gets the poker almost to a right-angle before relaxing the pressure. He holds the bent poker aloft for* HOLMES *and* WATSON *to see*]

See!

> [ROYLOTT *hurls the poker into the fireplace with a clatter*]

That's what I could do to you.

> [*He turns and strides to the door*]

See that you keep yourself out of my grip!

> [ROYLOTT *jerks open the door and exits, slamming it behind him.* WATSON *puts down his bottle and joins* HOLMES. *They laugh heartily*]

WATSON: I *say*, Holmes!

HOLMES: He seems a very amiable fellow!

> [HOLMES *saunters to the fireplace and picks up the poker to examine it*]

If he'd stayed a moment I might have shown him something.

> [HOLMES *suddenly takes a two-handed grip on the poker and, with a single jerk, bends it straight again.* WATSON *applauds*]

WATSON: Bravo, Holmes!

> [HOLMES *puts the poker back with the other fire-irons*]

'Scotland Yard Jack-in-Office', eh?

HOLMES: The insolence! Confusing *me* with the official police force!

WATSON: I hope he won't make that dear little lady suffer.

HOLMES: He's shown us that this is too serious a matter for any dawdling. Don't you see, Watson? His stepdaughters only come into their inheritance if they marry. One was about to do so, and died mysteriously two weeks beforehand. Now the other intends marriage, and the old, mysterious signs return.

WATSON: Serious business, all right.

HOLMES: I'll ring for our breakfast. By the way, Watson . . .

WATSON: Yes, Holmes?

HOLMES: I'd advise you to clean that old service revolver of yours. An Eley's No. 2 is an excellent argument with gentlemen who can twist steel pokers into knots.

[WATSON *goes at once to a drawer and opens it.*
HOLMES *rings the bell.* WATSON *turns with the revolver in his hand, breaks the breech and holds it up to the light to peer through the barrel.* Curtain]

SCENE TWO

[*This is played in front of a drop, painted to resemble the exterior of a country railway station, or simply in front of the lowered curtain.* HELEN *enters, right, as men and women – obviously passengers off a train – hurry away from left to exit right.* HELEN *peers past them and raises her hand to attract the attention of* HOLMES *and* WATSON, *as they enter left.* HOLMES *wears his ulster and deerstalker,* WATSON *his usual city clothes*]

HELEN: Mr. Holmes, Dr. Watson! I've been waiting so eagerly for your train.

[*They shake hands*]

WATSON: We meet again, Miss Stoner.

HOLMES: Is everything well with you, madam?

HELEN: It's all turned out splendidly. Dr. Roylott is away in town, as I expected. It's unlikely he'll be back before evening.

HOLMES: Oh, we had the pleasure of making the Doctor's acquaintance ourselves.

HELEN: Where?

[*She peers past them fearfully*]

In the train?

WATSON: He came to our rooms. Threw his weight about a bit, too. Trying to warn us off.

HELEN: He . . . he followed me there?

HOLMES: So it appears.

HELEN: What will he say when he returns?

HOLMES: He had better be on his guard. He may find there is someone more cunning than himself on *his* track.

HELEN: Then . . . Mr. Holmes, you really believe my stepfather has something to do with this mystery?

HOLMES: Judge for yourself, Miss Stoner. I found time before we left London to slip down to Doctors' Commons and examine your late mother's will. The total income left by her to your stepfather amounted to eleven hundred pounds a year, all derived from farm properties. But agricultural prices have fallen heavily since her death. The income has dwindled. I should say, to not much over seven hundred and fifty pounds.

HELEN: But what has this to do with anything?

HOLMES: Your mother stipulated that each daughter could claim an income of two hundred and fifty pounds a year in case of marriage. So, if both of you had married, your stepfather would have been left with what he might consider a pittance.

HELEN [*slowly*]: I see! Then . . . then even *one* marriage would reduce his income by about a third!

HOLMES: Exactly. My morning's work has proved that your stepfather has the strongest motives for standing in the way of your marriage. Your sister's marriage was prevented by some mysterious means, resulting in her death. And now . . . [*he breaks off*] Now, we must make the best use of our time. If you will kindly take us at once to the house?

HELEN: Of course. Please come this way, gentlemen.

[*She leads them off to exit right*]

SCENE THREE

[*A split set, representing the interiors of two adjoining bedrooms. In that to the audience's left hand, the bed is away from the dividing wall. A small safe stands in the corner, and there is a saucer on top of the safe. A wooden chair has its back to the back wall, in which a window is optional. A leather thong, or dog-whip, with its thin end knotted into a small loop, lies on the chair. An unlighted oil lamp stands on a bedside table. High up in the dividing wall is a ventilator. In the right-hand room, the bed – a metal, hospital type – stands against the dividing wall, with its foot to the audience. Dangling over it, attached to a point immediately above the ventilator in the dividing wall, is a bell-rope. A small table stands beside the bed, and there is a small chair near by. There is a window in the back wall, capable of opening and shutting.*

HOLMES, WATSON *and* HELEN, *attired as in the previous scene, stand in the right-hand room,* HOLMES *and* WATSON *looking about them*]

HOLMES: And this room, in which you are now sleeping, was formerly your late sister's?

HELEN: Yes. This . . . is where she met her death.

HOLMES [*pointing to the dividing wall*]: Dr. Roylott's room is next door in that direction?

HELEN: Yes. [*Pointing the other way*] My own room . . . my usual room, is that way.

HOLMES: I think you said you are sleeping here while alterations are going on?

HELEN: Well . . . I've looked into my room once or twice. No work seems to be in progress. No workmen have been here.

WATSON: Sounds like an excuse to get you to move into here.

HELEN: I had wondered . . .

HOLMES: Then let us examine this room. Now, as both you and your sister locked your doors at night, you were quite unapproachable from the corridor.

[HOLMES *points towards the audience*]

HELEN: Absolutely.

HOLMES: And the window was locked when your sister met her death?

[WATSON *goes to the window, handles the catch and tests it*]

HELEN: Yes.

WATSON: Perfectly firm. Couldn't budge that from outside.

HOLMES: Then, what else have we?

[*He spots the bell-rope*]

Bless my soul! A bell-rope!

HELEN: Yes. It rings in the housekeeper's room.

WATSON: Looks quite new. Didn't know they still made 'em.

HELEN: Oh, that one was only put in a couple of years ago.

HOLMES: Your sister asked for it, I suppose?

HELEN: No. I never heard of her using it. We always got what we needed for ourselves.

HOLMES: Indeed! Care to give it a tug, Watson?

WATSON: Certainly!

[*He goes to do so, then checks*]

What about the housekeeper? She'll hear it.

HELEN: It's all right. She's in the wash-house for the afternoon.

WATSON: Righto!

*[He tugs the rope, but there is no give in it and no
ring is heard. He tries again, with no result]*

That's funny!

[He tugs once more]

Doesn't seem to work. No give in it at all.

HOLMES: Let me see.

[He tugs the rope, then looks up to the top of it]

There's a simple explanation. This bell-rope is a dummy.

HELEN: A dummy? You mean, it won't ring?

HOLMES: It isn't even attached to a bell-wire.

WATSON: Strange, Holmes!

HOLMES: And interesting. Look – you can see it's fastened to
a hook, just above the little opening of the ventilator.

HELEN: I never noticed that before. How very absurd!

HOLMES: There are one or two seemingly absurd points
about this room. Have you noticed, for instance, that the
ventilator appears to connect with the adjoining room?

HELEN: I . . . Yes, I suppose it does!

WATSON: Take a fool of a builder to ventilate one room from
another, wouldn't it? Could just as easily have put it in the
outside wall.

HELEN [*nervously*]: The . . . the ventilator was a recent addi-
tion, too.

HOLMES: Done about the same time as the bell-rope, I fancy.

HELEN: Why, yes! There were several little changes about
that time.

HOLMES: They seem to have been of a most interesting
character. A dummy bell-rope and a ventilator that
doesn't ventilate! Ah, well! With your permission, Miss
Stoner, we shall now carry our researches into Dr
Roylott's own room.

HELEN [*apprehensively*]: Ce . . . certainly, Mr. Holmes.

c

[HELEN *leads the way 'out of the room' by approaching the audience and miming the opening of the door, which* WATSON, *bringing up the rear 'closes' after he has passed through.* HELEN *goes through the motions of opening* ROYLOTT'S *door to the next room, and they all go in,* WATSON *'closing the door' behind them.* HOLMES *glances round*]

HOLMES: Hm! Sparsely furnished, I see.

HELEN: It is, rather.

HOLMES: And a safe!

[*He goes to stand in front of the safe*]

What's in it?

HELEN: My stepfather's business papers.

HOLMES: You've seen inside it, then?

HELEN: Only once, some years ago. It was full of papers then.

HOLMES: There isn't a cat in it, for example?

WATSON: *Cat* in a *safe*, Holmes?

[HOLMES *picks up the saucer and shows it to them*]

HOLMES: Look at this. What's a saucer of milk doing here?

HELEN: I can't think. We don't keep a cat. But there's the cheetah – and the baboon.

HOLMES: Well, a cheetah is just a big cat, I suppose – and yet I dare say a saucer of milk would hardly satisfy its needs!

[HOLMES *replaces the saucer and looks at the chair. He picks up the leather thong*]

Hello! Here *is* something interesting!

WATSON: Looks like a dog-leash! That milk's for a dog, then.

HELEN: But we haven't a dog!

[HOLMES *catches up the looped end of the thong with his free hand and examines it closely,* WATSON *peering at it also*]

HOLMES: Tied to make a loop at the end. What do you make of that, Watson?

WATSON: Dashed if I know! Certainly wouldn't get a dog's neck through that. What d'you think, Holmes?

HOLMES: I think that it's a wicked world – and that when a clever man turns his brains to crime, it's wickedest of all. Now, I must just examine this chair.

[HOLMES *takes a magnifying glass from his pocket and peers through it at the seat of the chair.* WATSON *and* HELEN *exchange baffled glances.* HOLMES *straightens up and puts his glass away*]

Yes – that point's quite settled, then.

WATSON: Eh?

HOLMES [*seriously*]: Miss Stoner . . .

HELEN: Yes, Mr. Holmes?

HOLMES: It is essential that you should follow my advice in every single respect. Your life may depend on it.

HELEN: My . . . my life! I . . . I'm in your hands, Mr. Holmes.

HOLMES: In the first place, my friend and I must spend the night in your room.

HELEN [*horrified*]: Mr. Holmes!

HOLMES: Please allow me to explain. I believe the village inn is straight over there?

[*He points towards the window*]

HELEN: Yes – The Crown.

HOLMES: Your window should be visible from it, I think. Now, when your stepfather comes back, you must confine yourself to this room with a headache. Don't let him near you. You understand?

HELEN: Yes.

HOLMES: When you pretend to retire for the night, unfasten your window and shine a light from it as a signal to us. You must then withdraw quietly from the room and go and spend the night in the room you used to occupy. Could you manage to do that?

HELEN: Yes, easily. But what will you do?

HOLMES: We shall come over from the inn and spend the night in the room next to this. We shall investigate the cause of this whistling noise that has disturbed you.

HELEN: I see. Mr. . . . Mr. Holmes – I believe you have already made up your mind.

HOLMES: Perhaps I have.

HELEN: Then, for pity's sake, tell me what caused my sister's death!

HOLMES: I should prefer to have clearer proof before I speak. And now, Miss Stoner, we must leave you.

HELEN [*moving to the 'door'*] : Very well.

> [HELEN '*opens the door*' *and they follow her out,* WATSON '*closing*' *it*]

HOLMES: Miss Stoner – perhaps Dr. Watson and I should wait in your room for a moment, while you make sure the coast is clear for us to leave. If Dr. Roylott returned unexpectedly and found us, our journey would have been in vain.

HELEN: Please go in, then. I won't be a moment.

> [*She exits quickly, right.* HOLMES *and* WATSON *re-enter the right-hand room,* WATSON '*closing the door*']

WATSON: Well, Holmes?

HOLMES: You know, Watson, I really have some scruples about bringing you back here tonight. There's a distinct element of danger.

WATSON: Can I be of assistance?

HOLMES: Your presence might be invaluable.

WATSON: Then I shall certainly come!

[HOLMES *claps him on the shoulder*]

HOLMES: It's very kind of you.

WATSON: Holmes — you speak of danger. You've evidently seen more here than I have.

HOLMES: I imagine you've seen as much as I. But I fancy I've deduced a little more.

WATSON [*glancing round*]: I don't see anything remarkable — except that bell-rope.

HOLMES: You can see the ventilator, too.

WATSON: Yes — but, hang it, I don't think it's all *that* unusual to have a ventilator between two rooms!

HOLMES: Before we even came to Stoke Moran I knew we should find a ventilator.

WATSON: You did!

HOLMES: You remember in her statement she said that when she and her sister were talking in this room they could smell Roylott's cigar from next door?

WATSON: I remember.

HOLMES: The windows and doors were presumably closed — so I deduced a ventilator.

WATSON: Hah! Pretty obvious, I suppose.

HOLMES [*sarcastically*]: Oh, yes!

WATSON [*gazing at the ventilator*]: But what harm can there be in that?

HOLMES: At least there's a curious coincidence of dates. A ventilator is made, a bell-rope is hung, and a lady who sleeps in this room dies. By the way, did you notice anything peculiar about the bed?

WATSON: The bed?

[*He bends down to peer at the bed, and prods it tentatively*]

Can't see anything wrong with it.

HOLMES: It's clamped to the floor.

WATSON: What!

[*He examines the feet, then straightens up*]

Jove!

HOLMES: The bed can't be moved. It must always be in the same relative position to the ventilator and the bell-rope.

[WATSON'S *eyes travel from one thing to the other*]

WATSON: Holmes! Now I'm beginning to see!

HOLMES: Capital, my dear Watson!

WATSON: We . . . we're only just in time!

HOLMES: When a doctor does go wrong, Watson, he is the first of criminals. He has nerve and he has knowledge. Palmer and Pritchard were among the heads of their profession. This man strikes even deeper. But I think we shall be able to strike deeper still.

[HELEN *enters right*]

We shall have horrors enough before the night is over. So let's go and have a quiet pipe and turn our minds for a few hours to something more cheerful.

[HELEN *enters the room*]

HELEN: All clear, Mr. Holmes. You know the way to go.

HOLMES: Then good-bye, Miss Stoner – and be brave. If you do as I have told you, we shall soon drive away these dangers that threaten you.

[WATSON *nods to* HELEN. HOLMES *and* WATSON *leave the room and exit right, leaving her gazing hopefully after them. Blackout*]

SCENE FOUR

[The setting as before, only now the stage remains in darkness. All is still. After a few moments the glimmer of a bull's-eye lamp can be seen approaching from outside the window of the right-hand room. The window is opened and WATSON, *holding the lamp, climbs stealthily through, followed by* HOLMES, *who carries his walking-cane.* WATSON *closes the window. The stage lighting must now simulate the moderate illumination from their lamp — just sufficient to enable the details of the room to be seen and the action followed clearly. The left-hand room remains in complete darkness]*

WATSON: So far, so good!

HOLMES *[in a lowered voice]*: Keep your voice down, Watson. Just make sure she's locked the door securely.

*[*WATSON *goes through the motions of trying the door and turning a key]*

WATSON: She's left the key on the inside for us. I've locked it now.

HOLMES: Wise woman! Now, he's still in the parlour. I glimpsed him as we crossed the lawn. When he comes, he must believe Miss Stoner is in here, asleep.

WATSON: Hadn't we better sit in the dark?

HOLMES: I think not. It will be all right, so long as he can catch no glimmer through the ventilator.

*[*WATSON *places their lamp carefully on the bedside table. The bed and the bell-rope above it must be clearly seen, but the ventilator must remain in*

> shadow. HOLMES *draws out the small chair and places it facing the bed and the bell-rope*]

Watson, I will sit on the bed, and you in the chair.

> [WATSON *looks at the bed, and then, ruefully, at the hard chair*]

WATSON: Oh, all right!

> [*He sits on the chair.* HOLMES *sits near the foot of the bed*]

HOLMES: Don't go to sleep.

WATSON: Fat chance of that!

HOLMES: Your life may depend on it. Have your pistol ready, in case we should need it.

WATSON: Right.

> [*He draws his revolver and holds it on his knees.* HOLMES *keeps his cane in his hands. A smell of cigar-smoke becomes apparent*]

HOLMES: Now, is everything understood?

WATSON: So far. I only wish you'd tell me . . .

> [*He breaks off and sniffs*]

HOLMES [*lowering his voice further*]: What is it?

> [WATSON *sniffs again*]

WATSON [*low*]: A cigar! He's in there!

HOLMES: He'd enter silently and without a light, not to wake up Miss Stoner. Now, Watson, listen – and watch!

> [*They sit absolutely still and silent, their eyes towards the ventilator. After a few movements a snake-like hissing is heard from that direction. A snake begins to make its way down the bell-rope and stops half-way. There is a low whistle from the next room.* HOLMES *leaps up and lashes at the snake with his cane.* WATSON *jumps up, the snake slithers quickly up the bell-rope and out of sight*]

HOLMES [*shouting*] : You saw it, Watson? You saw it?

WATSON: I ... I think I ...

> [HOLMES *seizes the lamp and shines it at the*
> *ventilator, but the snake has disappeared,* ROY-
> LOTT, *in the next room, screams*]

HOLMES: Quickly, Watson! Roylott's room!

> [ROYLOTT *continues to scream. They rush to*
> *their door,* HOLMES *carrying the lamp.* WATSON
> '*unlocks the door' and they run to the left-hand*
> *room and run in. The stage lighting, simulating*
> *their lamp, reveals* ROYLOTT, *slumped silently on*
> *his chair with the snake coiled round his head and*
> *the leather thong dangling limply from his hand.*
> *The safe door is ajar*]

WATSON: Holmes! Round his head! A snake!

HOLMES: The band – the speckled band!

> [HOLMES *crosses carefully to* ROYLOTT]

It's a swamp adder – the deadliest snake in India! He's
dead already.

> [WATSON *approaches cautiously, his revolver at*
> *the ready*]

WATSON: Great heavens!

HOLMES: Violence does, in truth, recoil upon the violent.
The schemer falls into the pit which he digs for another.

WATSON: Never mind that, Holmes! Shall I shoot it?

HOLMES: No.

> [*He hands the lamp to* WATSON, *then moves*
> *carefully to* ROYLOTT *and takes the thong from*
> *his hand*]

This noose in the dog-leash will do it. It's obviously in-
tended for this.

> [HOLMES *carefully dangles the noose on to the*
> *snake, as though capturing it, then, with a swift*

> *movement, gathers the reptile up in his hands,*
> *holding it firmly by neck and tail]*

HOLMES: Quickly, Watson! The safe!

> [WATSON *hurriedly obeys, opening the safe door*
> *wide.* HOLMES *pops the snake inside and slams the*
> *door. They stand silently for a moment]*

WATSON: Whew!

> [HOLMES *draws out a handkerchief and mops his*
> *brow. Then, taking out a box of matches, he goes*
> *to the table-lamp and lights it. As the stage lights*
> *come up gradually to illuminate the whole room,*
> WATSON *blows their own lamp out and sets it*
> *down]*

HOLMES: You may put your trusty friend away, Watson. He won't be needed now.

> [WATSON *pats his revolver with a grin and re-*
> *turns it to his pocket.* HOLMES *subsides on to the*
> *bed.* WATSON *goes to* ROYLOTT *and examines*
> *him briefly]*

WATSON: He's dead, all right. But, Holmes – what made you suspect you'd find a snake?

HOLMES: When I examined Miss Stoner's room, it became clear to me that whatever danger threatened could not come either from the window or the door. The discovery that the bell-rope leading from near the ventilator was a dummy, and that her bed was clamped to the floor, instantly made me suspicious that the rope was there as a bridge.

WATSON: I thought as much!

HOLMES: The idea of a snake occurred to me at once. When I coupled it with the knowledge that Dr. Roylott was a fancier of creatures from India, I felt sure I was on the right track.

WATSON: I see!

HOLMES: The idea of using a form of poison which couldn't possibly be discovered by any chemical test was just what would occur to a clever and ruthless man with Eastern experience. It would be a sharp-eyed coroner who could distinguish two little dark punctures in the victim's skin.

WATSON: That's quite so. Miss Stoner didn't mention any such thing being found on her sister. But, then, what about the whistle? I heard it plainly.

HOLMES: So did I. You see, he would put the snake through the ventilator with the certainty that it would crawl down the rope and land on the bed. But he couldn't be sure that it would bite the occupant of the bed. She might escape every night for a week before she fell a victim. Therefore, he had to be able to recall the snake before the morning.

WATSON: By *whistling* to it?

HOLMES: The equivalent of the snake-charmer's flute. He probably trained it by means of that saucer of milk.

WATSON: Remarkable!

HOLMES: I had come to these conclusions before I even entered this room for the first time. You remember I examined the seat of that chair through my lens?

WATSON: Yes. What was that for?

HOLMES: Simply to confirm to myself that he had been in the habit of standing on it in order to reach the ventilator. When I saw the safe, the saucer of milk, and this loop of whipcord, any doubts I might still have had were dispelled.

WATSON [*slowly*]: Holmes . . .

HOLMES: Yes, my dear Watson?

WATSON: I'm rather glad I didn't know any of this before we settled down in that room next door. When I think of

that creature, sliding down the bell-rope towards us . . . !

HOLMES: Well, at least *I* sat on the bed and gave you the chair.

WATSON: So you did! And *you* knew what to expect!

HOLMES: As soon as I heard the creature hiss I knew for certain what we were up against. I don't mind admitting I was glad to use my stick on it.

WATSON: Did you *hope* to drive it back into here?

HOLMES: No, I wouldn't say that. Some of my blows got home and must have roused its snakish temper. It fled through the ventilator and fastened on the first person it saw.

> [HOLMES *gets to his feet and stands before* ROY-LOTT, *looking down at him*]

We must inform the country police of what has happened. No doubt I'm indirectly responsible for Dr. Grimesby Roylott's death – but I can't say it's likely to weigh very heavily upon my conscience.

> [*Curtain, as they stand contemplating the dead man*]

CHARLES AUGUSTUS MILVERTON

SCENE I: 221B Baker Street, *evening*
SCENE II: Near Hampstead Heath, *a day or two later*
SCENE III: Milverton's study, *evening, two days later*
SCENE IV: Regent Street: a photographer's window,
              next morning

Characters, in order of appearance:

DR. WATSON

SHERLOCK HOLMES

MRS. HUDSON

LADY EVA BRACKWELL: A debutante. Blonde, vivacious, petite, in her early twenties. Fashionably and expensively dressed.

MILVERTON: 'A man of fifty, with a large, intellectual head, a round, plump, hairless face, a perpetual frozen smile, and two keen grey eyes, which gleamed brightly from behind broad, gold-rimmed glasses. There was something of Mr. Pickwick's benevolence in his appearance, marred only by the insincerity of the fixed smile and by the hard glitter of those restless and penetrating eyes. His voice was as smooth and suave as his countenance.'

AGATHA: Milverton's housemaid. Early twenties, dark, flirtatious.

THE VEILED WOMAN: Tall, aristocratic, in her late twenties or early thirties.

INSPECTOR LESTRADE: 'A quick and energetic worker, despite his adherence to conventional methods to the exclusion of inspiration.' 'Sallow, rat-faced, dark-eyed . . .' In his forties. A rather rough accent.

CHARLES AUGUSTUS MILVERTON

SCENE ONE

[*The parlour of* 221B *Baker Street. The fire gleams dully and the lamp is turned low.* HOLMES AND WATSON *enter in outdoor clothes, having been walking on a frosty evening*]

WATSON: Ah! That's better, Holmes!

[*He goes straight to the fire and pokes it.* HOLMES *strips off his coat and throws it carelessly over a chair, then goes to the fire and stands before it, legs apart, lifting up his coat-tails to warm his behind.* WATSON *turns up the lamp, illuminating the room fully, before taking off his coat and muffler and hanging them, with his hat, carefully behind the door*]

HOLMES: I don't know which I enjoy more, my dear Watson – our little evening rambles, or the agreeable home-coming when they're over.

WATSON: Well, we've Mrs. Hudson to thank for this part of it.

[*He returns to the fire, sits, and proceeds to take off his boots, extending his toes to the fire and wiggling the warmth into them*]

A good fire, the lamp lit, our slippers waiting . . .

[*He draws on his slippers*]

HOLMES: Bliss, Watson, bliss! It makes me feel festive. I might even give you a tune.

WATSON [*mock dismay*]: You're not going to play that fiddle!

HOLMES: Fiddle! Are you referring to my Stradivarius?

[*Knock at the door*]

WATSON [*chuckling*] : Come in!

[MRS. HUDSON *enters and approaches*]

Ah, Mrs. Hudson! We were just congratulating you *in absentia*. You make us very comfortable.

MRS. HUDSON: It's very civil of you to say so, Dr. Watson, I'm sure.

HOLMES: You mustn't spoil my friend, Mrs. Hudson. He'll start growing fat and lazy.

[MRS. HUDSON *catches sight of* HOLMES'S *street things thrown carelessly down. With an impatient little toss of the head she goes to gather them up and hang them neatly beside* WATSON'S]

MRS. HUDSON: It's you who could do with some fat on your ribs, Mr. Holmes. If you'd only eat your meals regularly like Dr. Watson.

[WATSON *makes a face at* HOLMES *behind her back.* HOLMES *winks broadly. This is an old familiar lecture.* WATSON *chuckles aloud.* MRS. HUDSON *wheels on him, more in sorrow than in anger*]

I'm surprised at a medical gentleman like you permitting it, Dr. Watson.

[WATSON *cowers back into his chair*]

WATSON [*hastily*] : Oh, I quite agree! It's disgraceful!

MRS. HUDSON: That's exactly what I mean, Doctor! I think . . . Oh!

[*Her hands fly to her mouth in dismay*]

WATSON [*sitting up*] : What's the matter?

MRS. HUDSON: I do beg pardon, Mr. Holmes. There's a visitor to see you.

[HOLMES *stretches indolently*]

HOLMES [*mock sorrow*]: And just as I was about to call for a nice juicy beefsteak!

MRS. HUDSON: Oh, go on with you now, sir! Shall I show the lady up?

HOLMES: A lady?

MRS. HUDSON: A real one, sir. Lady Eva Brackwell.

HOLMES [*dropping the banter*]: Please show Lady Eva up at once, Mrs. Hudson.

MRS. HUDSON [*the game over*]: Very well, sir.

[*She exits, closing the door*]

WATSON: That's spared me your fiddle recital, at any rate.

HOLMES: Do you know her, Watson?

WATSON [*puzzling*]: Lady Eva Brackwell? Name's familiar ... Ah, I know! Debutante. Going to marry ...

[*He is interrupted by a knock on the door, which opens, revealing* MRS. HUDSON]

MRS. HUDSON: Lady Eva Brackwell, sir.

[*She steps back out of sight as* LADY EVA *enters the room. The door closes.* LADY EVA *extends her hand to* HOLMES]

HOLMES: How do you do, Lady Eva?

LADY EVA: Mr. Holmes.

HOLMES: Allow me to present my friend and associate, Dr. Watson.

LADY EVA: How do you do?

WATSON [*shaking her hand*]: Charmed, my lady. Will you take the basket chair?

[*He pushes it forward for her*]

LADY EVA: Thank you. Mr. Holmes, I have only a few moments ...

WATSON: If you'd like me to leave, Holmes ...?

D

HOLMES: No, no – with Lady Eva's permission. You may speak freely before my friend, madam.

LADY EVA: Very well. Mr. Holmes, I must first apologize to you for calling here unannounced. The matter is too urgent for any delay.

[HOLMES *waves aside her apology*]

You may perhaps have heard my name?

[HOLMES *inclines his head*]

The fact is that I am engaged to be married to the Earl of Dovercourt in a fortnight's time – the eighteenth, to be exact.

WATSON: May I offer my congratulations?

LADY EVA: Thank you, Dr. Watson. [*Bashfully*] Unfortunately . . .

HOLMES: Yes?

LADY EVA: There are some – letters.

HOLMES: Pray go on, madam.

LADY EVA [*with a rush*]: Mr. Holmes, before I met my future husband I wrote some letters to a – a young man: a country squire. Looking back, I realize they were – imprudent. Nothing more, believe me, Mr. Holmes; but enough to break off my present match.

HOLMES: I see. Do I understand that the letters are now in the Earl of Dovercourt's possession?

LADY EVA: No, heaven forbid! But they may soon be.

HOLMES: How so?

LADY EVA: Mr. Holmes, yesterday I had a visit from a Mr. Milverton . . .

HOLMES [*almost shouting*]: Milverton!

LADY EVA: Oh! You know him?

HOLMES: Yes, I know Mr. Charles Augustus Milverton. Very well indeed. And he knows me!

LADY EVA: He never said so.

HOLMES [*shrugging*] : Why should he mention my name?

LADY EVA: I told him I should visit you. Yes, now I remember! He smiled! That horrible smile!

HOLMES: Tell me, Lady Eva – how much is he asking for the return of your letters?

LADY EVA: Then you've seen him already?

HOLMES: No, no. I assure you. But from what you have told me of the nature of the letters, coupled with your forthcoming marriage and a visit from Milverton, there is only one conclusion to be drawn.

LADY EVA [*urgently*] : Mr. Holmes, how he gained possession of them I cannot say. He wouldn't tell me. But he has them – he showed me one of them. His own words were, 'If the money is not paid on the fourteenth there certainly will be no marriage on the eighteenth.' He was horrible: so polite and well mannered, yet so, so . . .

HOLMES: I know exactly. You have my deepest sympathy. But I must ask you again – how much?

LADY EVA [*swallows*] : Seven thousand pounds.

WATSON: Seven thousand!

HOLMES [*smacking his fist angrily into his palm*] : You haven't paid him?

LADY EVA: No!

HOLMES: You are quite right.

LADY EVA: I *can't* pay such a man.

HOLMES: It's out of the question.

LADY EVA: But what am I to do?

HOLMES [*controlling his anger*] : What did you tell Milverton?

LADY EVA: I said that I must have time. I wanted to get rid of him before my father found him about the house. I begged him not to come there again. He said he would

be prepared to deal through an intermediary, if I preferred, and for no reason at all I suddenly thought of your name.

HOLMES: You came to the right person, Lady Eva. But this happened yesterday. Why did you not come to me sooner?

LADY EVA: I couldn't get away from Mama. I've had to spend all day trailing about the shops buying my trousseau, unable to slip away and knowing all the time that unless some miracle happens there will be no need for a trousseau at all.

WATSON: You're sure you can't confide in your future husband?

LADY EVA: Absolutely. He has – strong views. Mr. Holmes, I had to see you this evening at all costs because Milverton will be coming here, and you would have been unprepared.

HOLMES: He's coming this evening?

LADY EVA: He said so. I hope you don't think too badly of me, giving him your name without consulting you. I – I had to do something.

HOLMES: Not at all. Lady Eva, it is painful for me to have to say this, but from my knowledge of Milverton and his habits I warn you that there may be no alternative to paying him.

LADY EVA [becoming emotional]: But I can't! I haven't nearly enough. I couldn't hope to raise more than half at the most.

HOLMES: I understand. Even that might be sufficient – for the moment. Our immediate purpose must be to ensure that nothing arises to prevent the marriage taking place. If we can get Milverton to agree to taking a portion now, in return for staying his hand temporarily, we shall have more time to see what can be done next.

WATSON: Holmes, you're surely not going to . . . It's blackmail!

HOLMES: I haven't much taste for it, Watson, believe me. Knuckling under to a blackmailer is not my preference. But if we refuse him now, we lose all. Better to play for time.

WATSON: Well, I suppose you're right.

HOLMES: Lady Eva, you may leave the matter with me. I'll see Milverton and try to make the best terms I can for the time being. Meanwhile, pray proceed with your wedding arrangements as though nothing were amiss. Life's crises come and go. Let us not submit to this one until we have no alternative.

LADY EVA [*rising*]: Thank you, thank you, Mr. Holmes. Your name came to me like an inspiration. I can't tell you how glad I am.

HOLMES [*leading her to the door*]: If Milverton gets in touch with you again refuse to see him. Tell him you will only deal through me.

LADY EVA [*at door*]: Very well. Good evening, Mr. Holmes – Dr. Watson.

WATSON [*leaping forward to open the door*]: Good evening, dear lady.

> [LADY EVA *exits*. WATSON *closes door.*
> HOLMES *returns to the fire, chin in hand, deep in*
> *thought.* WATSON *follows*]

WATSON: This Milverton . . .

HOLMES [*jerked into mounting anger*]: The worst man in London! When you stand before the serpents in the Zoo, and see the slithery, gliding, venomous creatures, don't you feel a creeping, shrinking sensation?

> [WATSON *shudders*]

Well, that's how Milverton impresses me. I've had to do

with fifty murderers in my career, but the worst of them
never gave me the repulsion I have for this fellow.

WATSON: But who is he?

> [*The shadows creep forward a little as the light
> diminishes*]

HOLMES: He's the king of all the blackmailers. Heaven help
the man – and still more the woman – whose secret and
reputation come into Milverton's power. With a smiling
face and a heart of marble he'll squeeze and squeeze
until he's drained them dry.

WATSON: How does he work?

HOLMES: He allows it to be known that he's prepared to pay
very high sums for letters which will compromise people
of wealth or position. He finds plenty of takers – valets,
maids, and those artful 'gentlemen' who've won the
affection of trusting women.

WATSON: And *does* he pay well?

HOLMES: Extremely. I happen to know that he once paid a
footman £700 for a note just two lines in length. It
brought the ruin of a noble family.

> [WATSON *whistles*]

Oh, yes. Everything of that kind that's in the market
goes to Milverton eventually. I tell you, Watson, there
are hundreds – literally hundreds – in this city who'd
turn white if you mentioned his name to them. None of
them knows just when he might put the grip on them.
He'll hold a card back for years in order to play it at the
moment when the stakes are highest.

WATSON: But surely the police can do something about
him?

HOLMES [*walking up and down*]: Evidence, Watson, evidence.
Where's the woman who'd risk her own ruin just to get
him a few months in prison? He's cunning; a genius in

his way. He never blackmails an innocent person. The day he makes that mistake, they'll have him.

WATSON [*sighing*]: I see. Then what . . .

[*He is interrupted by a knock at the door and* MRS. HUDSON'S *entry*]

HOLMES: Yes, Mrs. Hudson?

MRS. HUDSON: A Mr. Milverton to see you, Mr. Holmes.

[HOLMES *and* WATSON *exchange glances*]

HOLMES: I'll see him at once.

MRS. HUDSON [*going*]: Yes, sir. [*Pausing at door*] What time should I serve dinner, sir?

HOLMES [*abstracted*]: Eh? Oh, no dinner for me, Mrs. Hudson. I – I seem to have lost my appetite.

WATSON: Same here.

[MRS. HUDSON *considers a protest, but changes her mind, shrugs resignedly and goes out, closing the door*]

WATSON [*urgently*]: What are you going to do, Holmes?

[HOLMES *presses his fingertips to his forehead. He does not answer*]

Holmes?

HOLMES [*on a sigh*]: The best I can, my dear Watson.

[*Knock at door.* MRS. HUDSON *enters*]

MRS. HUDSON: Mr. Milverton, sir.

[MILVERTON *enters and she retreats, closing the door.* MILVERTON *stands, slowly looking from* HOLMES *to* WATSON *and back again, wearing his perpetual smile. He advances slowly and extenps his hand to* HOLMES, *who ignores it.* MILVERTON'S *smile broadens. He slowly removes his astrakhan-collared overcoat, folds it with great deliberation, and places it carefully over the back of a chair. He seats himself in a fireside chair and sinks*

> *back at his ease, looking up at the frigid* HOLMES
> *and glowering* WATSON]

MILVERTON: Well, Mr. Holmes?

HOLMES [*controlling himself with some difficulty*]: Well – Milverton?

MILVERTON [*indicating Watson without looking at him*]: This gentleman?

> [WATSON *draws himself up in a military stance*]

HOLMES: Dr. Watson is my friend and partner.

MILVERTON [*benignly*]: Oh, I was merely thinking of your client's interests.

> [*He beams at* WATSON]

The matter is so very – delicate . . .

> [HOLMES *grabs for his pipe and tobacco from the
> mantelpiece and proceeds to calm himself by filling
> the pipe and lighting it during the following*]

HOLMES: Dr. Watson has already heard the particulars.

MILVERTON [*sighing*]: So very, very delicate . . . But shall we proceed to business? I understand you are acting for Lady Eva?

HOLMES: I am.

MILVERTON: And has she empowered you to accept my terms?

HOLMES: What are they?

MILVERTON [*as though surprised*]: Seven thousand pounds.

HOLMES [*with an attempt at casualness*]: And the alternative?

MILVERTON: My dear sir, it is painful to me to discuss it.

> [HOLMES *lights his pipe and puffs it up before
> speaking again*]

HOLMES: You're taking rather a lot for granted.

> [MILVERTON *raises his eyebrows*]

My client will do what I advise.

MILVERTON: Which is?

HOLMES: To tell her future husband the whole story, and trust to his generosity.

[MILVERTON *chuckles*]

MILVERTON: Evidently you don't know the earl.

[*He savours the thought before going on*]
The letters are sprightly – very sprightly. The lady was a charming correspondent. But I'm sure the Earl of Dovercourt wouldn't appreciate that.

[*He sighs*]
Still, since you think otherwise, we'll let it rest at that.

[*He prepares to rise*]
If you think it in your client's best interests that the letters should be placed in the earl's hands, then I quite agree – it would be foolish to pay so much money to get them back.

[*He half rises*]

HOLMES [*hastily*]: Wait a moment!

[HOLMES *puts aside his pipe.* MILVERTON *remains half-way out of his chair*]
You're going too fast. We – we must ensure there is no scandal.

[MILVERTON *sinks back again, smiling broadly*]

MILVERTON: I was sure you'd see it in that light.

HOLMES: At the same time, Lady Eva isn't a wealthy woman.

[MILVERTON *nods agreement*]
Even two thousand pounds would be a great drain on her resources. Still – if you will moderate your demands I could guarantee you that sum.

MILVERTON: You're quite right, of course, Mr. Holmes. She hasn't much money.

HOLMES: Then . . .

MILVERTON: At the same time, you must admit that the occasion of a lady's marriage is a very suitable moment for her friends and relatives to make some little – effort – on her behalf?

[WATSON *cannot suppress a snort of anger.* MILVERTON *turns and addresses the rest of his speech to him*]

MILVERTON: Imagine, Doctor – even now they may be in difficulties over the choice of a suitable wedding present for her. Well, let me assure them that this little bundle of letters would give more joy than all the candelabra and butter-dishes in London.

WATSON: Pah!

[*He turns his back on* MILVERTON, *who sighs*]

HOLMES: It's out of the question, Milverton.

MILVERTON: Dear me, dear me! How unfortunate! You know, I can't help feeling that ladies in such a situation ought to make some little effort.

[*He draws an envelope from his inner pocket and holds it up towards* HOLMES]

See this? Look at the coat of arms.

[WATSON *cannot prevent himself turning round to see*]

It belongs to . . . Well, perhaps it wouldn't be fair to mention the name before tomorrow morning. By then, Mr. Holmes, it will be in a certain lady's husband's hands. Oh, yes. And all because she won't find a beggarly sum which wouldn't take her an hour, if she'd turn her diamonds into paste. It's such a pity, really.

[WATSON *steps forward, as though he might snatch the envelope from him.* MILVERTON *smiles at him and stows it safely away.* WATSON *looks appealingly at* HOLMES]

HOLMES: Listen to me. The money simply can't be found.

Surely, it's better for you to take the two thousand she can offer? It's a substantial sum. If you ruin her instead you get nothing.

MILVERTON: Ah, now there you make a mistake. An exposure would be even more profitable – indirectly, that is.

WATSON: I don't see how.

MILVERTON: Because I have eight or ten other cases, shall we say, maturing? It only needs to be known that I made a severe example of the Lady Eva . . . Why, I should find the others much more open to reason.

HOLMES [*suddenly*]: Very well, Milverton. Watson – lock the door!

> [WATSON *springs to do so.* MILVERTON *rises surprisingly quickly to his feet, at the same time whipping out a revolver, which he points at* HOLMES. *He steps carefully aside, until, with his back to the fire, he can observe both of them. All three freeze in this attitude for a moment, then* MILVERTON *breaks the suspense with silent laughter*]

MILVERTON: Mr. Holmes, Mr. Holmes! I've been expecting you to do something original. This has been done so often before. You really disappoint me.

> [MILVERTON *moves carefully to where his coat lies*]

Don't mistake me. I'm perfectly ready to use this. The law would protect me. Unlawful detention, don't you know?

> [*He scoops up his coat with his free arm*]

In any case, you don't suppose I'd bring the letters with me, do you? Nothing so foolish.

> [*He moves towards the door, gesturing* WATSON *out of the way with the gun*]

And now, gentlemen, I have one or two more interviews this evening, so if you'll excuse me . . .?

[*He wriggles into the coat, contriving all the time to keep the revolver free for use. It appears that* WATSON *might jump at him, but no chance arises*]

You have until the fourteenth, Mr. Holmes. You know where to find me – Appledore Towers, Hampstead.

[*He opens the door behind his back, and, deftly pocketing the revolver at the same time, bows and slips out, closing the door.* WATSON *snatches up the nearest blunt instrument and makes for the door*]

HOLMES: No, Watson!

[WATSON *checks and looks round in surprise*]

Let him go.

[WATSON *hesitates, then obediently lays down his weapon and rejoins* HOLMES *in front of the fire*]

WATSON: I'd have cracked his skull!

HOLMES [*sinking into his fireside chair*]: It would have done us no good. It was foolish of me to lose my temper. You can be sure those letters are safe somewhere, with arrangements made for their delivery into the wrong hands if anything happened to him.

WATSON: I suppose so. But, Holmes – what's to be done?

HOLMES [*wearily*]: I don't know, Watson, I don't know at all.

[*He gets to his feet and finds his neglected pipe*]

Are you going out, my dear Watson?

WATSON [*about to sit*]: Out? No!

HOLMES: As you pass the tobacconist's you might tell him to send me up a pound of the strongest shag?

[*He commences lighting his pipe*]

This is more than any three-pipe problem. But the

answer will come, Watson. Let's hope it doesn't take too long, that's all.

[WATSON *grins, walks smartly to the door and takes down his coat and hat. As he opens the door he looks back at* HOLMES, *but sees that he is already deep in thought, his chin sunk on his chest and his pipe billowing clouds of smoke.* WATSON *exits as the stage lighting dims out, leaving only the dull glow of the fire*]

[*A brief pause, to denote passage of time, then gradually bring up the stage lighting.* HOLMES *is in the same attitude as before, only now wreathed about thickly by tobacco smoke. He puffs on motionlessly for a few moments, then, suddenly, jerks the pipe out of his mouth, tosses his head triumphantly, and springs to his feet. He lays the pipe aside and goes swiftly to the bureau, opening a drawer and taking out a few objects. He strips off his jacket, throws it aside, and, with his back to the audience, dons a walrus moustache, a quiff of hair, a pair of false eyebrows, and fills out his cheeks with cotton-wool pads. While he is thus engaged,* WATSON *enters and immediately starts coughing and wafting with his hat at the pipe smoke.* HOLMES *does not look up*]

WATSON: Great heavens, Holmes! Wonder you don't suffocate. Ugh!

HOLMES [*back to audience*]: I suppose it is rather thick, now you mention it.

WATSON: Thick! You must have smoked the whole blessed tin!

HOLMES: Ah, but it brought its result.

WATSON: It did?

HOLMES: Yes.

[*As he speaks he turns to face* WATSON *and the audience, revealing the disguise he has been*

*assuming. The desired effect is of a rather dashing,
but eminently clean-living Victorian working man.
He beams at* WATSON]

WATSON: Great heavens!

[*As* WATSON *stands gaping,* HOLMES *sticks his
thumbs in his waistcoat armholes, spreads his
fingers and begins to strut to and fro in a cocky
manner*]

Holmes! What on earth . . .?

HOLMES [*singing in exaggerated Cockney*]: 'She was as beautiful
as a butterfly, and as prahd as a queen, was Pretty Little
Polly Perkins of Paddington Green-ah!'

WATSON [*laughing heartily*]: Holmes, I don't know how you
do it! Who – who are you supposed to be?

HOLMES [*still Cockney*]: Name of Escott, guv'nor. Rising
young plumber – and a bachelor still!

[*He winks hugely*]

WATSON: I see, I see. And tell me, for whose benefit is all
this?

HOLMES [*reverting to his own voice*]: For the housemaid at
Appledore Towers, Hampstead.

WATSON: Milverton's place!

HOLMES: The same. And I only hope she's susceptible to a
little charm.

WATSON: Charm? You, Holmes!

[*He chortles*]

HOLMES: You'd hardly call me a marrying man, would
you?

WATSON: I would not!

HOLMES: No. Still, needs must, when the Devil drives. And
Milverton's all the Devil I need to spur me on, Watson.

[*He begins to bustle about again*]

Come on, it's late enough already. Help me find those old clothes I keep in the attic and speed me on my way.

[*Watson hurries to the door*]

WATSON: Right, Holmes.

[*He pauses as he opens it*]

And only a few hours ago you were carrying on about unscrupulous men winning the affections of trusting women! I'm surprised, Holmes. Surprised!

[*He goes out grinning.* HOLMES *begins to unbutton his waistcoat and peel it off as the curtain falls*]

SCENE TWO

[*This is played in front of a drop, painted to represent a Hampstead scene – part of the heath, or a Victorian or earlier façade, for instance – or in front of the curtain.* HOLMES, *fully disguised as 'Escott', enters from right and takes up a stance, waiting for* AGATHA. *He adjusts his collar, gives his jacket a tug or two, swishes his cane, etc.* AGATHA *enters left, approaching* HOLMES *rather coyly, as he springs to attention and doffs his jaunty bowler*]

HOLMES [*as Escott*]: Well, Miss Agatha!

[*She extends her hand politely and he shakes it*]

AGATHA: How d'you do, Mr. Escott?

HOLMES: Very nicely, I'm sure. [*With a wink*] All the better for seeing you again.

AGATHA [*giggles*]: Oh, get on! I nearly didn't come, you know.

HOLMES: Oho!

AGATHA: No. A girl has to be careful on Hampstead Heath.

HOLMES: And so has a feller!

AGATHA: Silly! I mean, I hardly know you – 'cept from the other night when you came to Mr. Milverton's about the gas leak that wasn't.

HOLMES [*scratching his neck*]: Funny thing, that. I could've swore I had the right address. Still, never mind that. Shall we – er – take a stroll?

AGATHA: Suits me.

[*They move off slowly to the left, talking as they disappear into the wings*]

HOLMES: Very nice spot to be in service, Hampstead, I should've said. Very select.

AGATHA: Oh, very. Not like my last place at Paddington. Never knew what you was going to see going on in the street there.

[*They are now out of sight. After a few seconds they reappear, slowly crossing the stage from left to right*]

HOLMES: Yes, Kentish Town. That's where my little place is.

AGATHA: I got an auntie in Kentish Town. Getting built up, though, isn't it?

HOLMES: Not my bit. Got a little back garden – room for a few fowls. Nice kitchen with a back boiler – put it in myself, that boiler.

[*They pause in mid-stage*]

AGATHA: A good boiler keeps the house warm real nice, I always think. Cosy.

HOLMES: Ah, yes. [*He sighs*] 'Ome, Sweet 'Ome. Now, when I get an apprentice, like I shall soon, I shall have more time at 'ome.

AGATHA: That's nice, then.

HOLMES [*leaning a little towards her*]: Mind, it ain't no use being at 'ome if there's no – Little Woman there as well.

[AGATHA *averts her face coyly*]

No slippers in the fender, no bright fire waiting. No, I don't go much on that lark.

AGATHA: Well, never mind. Perhaps one day Miss Right'll come along.

HOLMES [*digging her in the ribs*]: Perhaps she has – eh?

AGATHA [*very dignified*]: Now then, Mr. Escott! Such talk!

HOLMES: Why? You aren't spoken for, are you?

E

AGATHA: You ask Ben Wrigley that.

HOLMES: Who's he, when he's at home?

AGATHA: He works for our butcher. Got a nasty temper, too.

[*They resume their stroll*]
You'd better not let him see you hanging round me, that's all.

[*She giggles*]

HOLMES: Well, let me tell you, I *eat* butchers' boys for breakfast – half a dozen every morning regular, so he'd better not get too close when I've got my appetite up!

AGATHA [*laughing*]: Ooh! You're a card – a real card, aren't you?

[*They are off stage by now. After a few seconds they reappear, now strolling right to left*]

HOLMES: I reckon I saw your master once – Mr. what's-his-name?

AGATHA: Milverton.

HOLMES: That's it. Yes. Fond of his food, I'd say.

AGATHA: You just ask Cook!

HOLMES: Good eater – sound *sleeper*, eh?

AGATHA: Sleep? Why, he wouldn't hear the Guards Band play 'Rule Britannia' under his window.

[*They pause in mid-stage*]

HOLMES [*thoughtfully*]: Good!

AGATHA: Good?

HOLMES [*quickly*]: Good *for* him, I mean. Works hard, after all, I dare say?

AGATHA: Always at it. Even at home. He has a study, just next to his bedroom.

HOLMES: You don't say! Still, just the place to keep his safe, where he can always have his eye on it. Stands to sense, I mean.

AGATHA [*her attention wandering*] : That's right.

HOLMES : Be easy to burgle, though – him sleeping that heavy.

AGATHA : I dunno about that. There's Prince.

HOLMES : Prince?

AGATHA : Yes. A great big black dog he keeps. Ever so fierce.

HOLMES [*gloomily*] : Oh!

AGATHA : He doesn't frighten me, though. Eats out of my hand.

HOLMES : Hence the saying 'Lucky Dog'.

AGATHA : There – you're at it again, Mr. Escott!

HOLMES : Well, Miss Agatha, I won't say I wasn't going to ask if I could call round the back for you – the night after tomorrow, perhaps? Still, now you mention that dog, I reckon I'd better change me mind. Got chased by one when I was a nipper. Nasty!

AGATHA [*hastily*] : Oh, he wouldn't get after you.

HOLMES : Well, I couldn't be sure of that, could I?

AGATHA : I – tell you what. I could lock him up.

HOLMES : You could?

AGATHA : He's supposed to have the run of the grounds, in case of burglars. But if I locked him up for an hour or two I don't reckon he'd be missed.

HOLMES : Now you're talking – Agatha.

> [*She simpers.* HOLMES *offers his arm. She takes it and they stroll off jauntily to the left,* HOLMES *swinging his cane and whistling* 'Pretty Polly Perkins of Paddington Green']

SCENE THREE

[MILVERTON'S *study by night. A lamp burns on a low flame. There is a door, back left, and french windows, with their curtains drawn shut, back right. Between the door and windows stands a safe. A desk and chair occupy the extreme left of the set, so as not to obscure the action at the back. A few books, and perhaps a globe, will serve to denote a study. After a few moments the curtains are parted stealthily and* HOLMES – *now in his own clothes, but wearing a black mask – peers cautiously round the room. Satisfied, he motions behind him with his hand and enters the room carrying a small hand-bag, followed by* WATSON, *also masked, who pulls the french windows to behind him, but does not fasten them*]

HOLMES [*quietly, but not too low*] : So far, Watson, so good.

[*He removes his mask and turns up the lamp a little*]

WATSON: Better take care, Holmes!

HOLMES: It's all right, my dear fellow. He'll be at dinner, at the other end of the house. Always is at this time – so my little informant assures me.

[WATSON *chuckles as he removes his hat and mask*]

WATSON: You know, Holmes, it really is a bit thick!

HOLMES: My dear Watson, I do wish you'd let my scruples alone. The information I needed was vital.

WATSON: Yes, but that poor girl!

HOLMES: Poor me, you mean! I've walked out with her

evening after evening. I've talked with her. [*He groans*]:
Oh dear, those talks!

WATSON [*chuckling*]: Serve you right! Now you're going to
drop her like a hot brick, I suppose?

HOLMES: She's told me all I need to know. She's got that dog
under lock and key, on the off-chance that I might be
paying her one of my evening visits. Faithful little Aggie!
Perhaps a box of handkerchiefs through the post,
wouldn't you say?

WATSON: I'd say you were an out-and-out bounder – if I
didn't know you as well as I do.

HOLMES: When such stakes are on the table we must play
our cards as best we can. [*Brightening*] Anyway, you'll
rejoice to know that her affections were already swing-
ing back noticeably towards my rival, the butcher's
boy. I fancy the young lady will survive the disappoint-
ment.

WATSON: Ah, well – hadn't we better get on?

> [HOLMES *crosses to the desk and places his bag on
> it*]

HOLMES: You know, I've always thought I'd have made a
thoroughly efficient criminal.

> [*He snaps open the bag and produces a jemmy,
> which he brandishes.* WATSON *goes over to look*]

Isn't it a beauty? A first-class, up-to-date burgling outfit.

> [*He produces tools as he speaks*]

Nickel-plated jemmy, diamond-tipped glass-cutter,
skeleton keys – every modern improvement called for by
the march of civilization.

WATSON: You got those french windows open easily enough.

HOLMES: Elementary. Now, Watson, just for safety's sake,
you stand by the door and listen. If you hear the

slightest sound, get behind the curtains as quickly as you can, and keep still.

WATSON: Very well.

> [*He takes up a stance at the door and listens intently at it, while* HOLMES *replaces his tools in his bag, crosses to the safe and kneels to it, with his bag beside him*]

Not a sound just now.

HOLMES: He likes his food, does the master.

> [*He begins work on the safe door*]

Never gets up from table before nine, I'm told.

> [WATSON *glances at his watch*]

WATSON: Not quite half past eight. Think you can do it in half an hour?

HOLMES: Nothing simpler. Either Milverton's too mean to buy a more up-to-date safe, or he's becoming careless.

> [*He grunts with effort, as he forces with the jemmy*]

One way or the other, he's left our task much easier.

> [*There is a sound of metal giving.* HOLMES *swings the safe door open.*]

There!

WATSON [*moving towards him*]: Bravo, Holmes!

HOLMES: Not quite my fastest time, but a good attempt.

WATSON [*peering into the safe*]: Letters! Bundles of them.

HOLMES: Possibly his whole hoard.

WATSON: Going to take the lot?

> [HOLMES *begins to stuff bundles of letters into his bag*]

HOLMES: I fancy we shall be doing a number of people a service.

> [*He pauses suddenly and cocks his ear*]

Listen, Watson!

[WATSON *takes a silent stride back towards the door and listens*]

WATSON: Someone's coming!

HOLMES: Confound it!

[*He springs to his feet, picking up his bag and pushing the safe door shut. He motions to* WATSON, *who slips across and behind the curtains.* HOLMES *glances round quickly, turns the lamp lower, then follows* WATSON. *They conceal themselves. After a few seconds the room door opens and* MILVERTON *comes slowly in, clad in a smoking jacket. He hums contentedly to himself. He closes the door, goes to the lamp and turns it up, then moves one or two papers on his desk. He takes out his watch and looks at it, then goes towards the safe. He is just reaching his hand out towards the safe door handle, when there is a knock at the door.* MILVERTON *turns away from the safe as* AGATHA, *dressed in her maid's uniform, enters*]

AGATHA: Beg pardon, sir.

MILVERTON: Yes, my dear?

AGATHA: There's a person called to see you, sir. A woman.

MILVERTON: Ah!

AGATHA: Won't give no – any name, sir. I don't know who she is.

MILVERTON [*beaming*]: That's all right, Agatha. I'm expecting her. Show her straight along.

AGATHA [*going*]: Very good, sir.

[*She exits, leaving the door slightly open.* MIL-VERTON *turns towards the safe, but changes his mind and goes back to the desk. He opens a drawer and takes out a wad of money, which he riffles through, then replaces, shutting the drawer.* AGATHA *returns*]

AGATHA: The – person, sir.

> [*She stands aside to let a veiled woman enter the room, then goes out, closing the door.* MILVERTON *moves to meet the woman*]

MILVERTON [*crossly*] : You're late. I said half past eight.

WOMAN [*an uneducated accent*] : I – I'm sorry, sir. I come as soon as I could get away.

> [MILVERTON *beams and pats her arm. She draws it away convulsively, but he overlooks this*]

MILVERTON: Never mind, never mind. Let's hope you'll prove worth the waiting for, eh?

WOMAN: Yes, sir.

MILVERTON: That countess must be a hard mistress to you, I dare say?

WOMAN: Sir.

MILVERTON [*rubbing his hands together*] : Well, then, here's your chance to get even with her – eh?

> [*He senses that the woman is tense*]

Why, bless me, girl, what are you shivering about? You'll probably be a rich woman in a minute or two.

WOMAN: I'm – I'm all right, sir.

MILVERTON: Good. Then let's get to business. I understand you've got five letters written by the Countess d'Albert which you think'll interest me. That right?

WOMAN: Yes.

MILVERTON: You want to sell them. I want to buy them. So far, so good. All there is to do is to fix a price.

WOMAN [*her voice hardening and losing some of its accent*] : That's all.

MILVERTON: Of course, I shall have to inspect the letters first. You have them there?

WOMAN [*opening her handbag*] : Yes.

MILVERTON [*beaming; quite unsuspecting*] : And I may as well inspect you at the same time. I fancy you're a pretty little thing under all this.

> [*He raises his hand to lift her veil. She withdraws a small revolver from her bag and pushes him away with it*]

WOMAN [*her own, cultured voice*] : Get back from me, Milverton!

> [*He retreats a pace or two*]

MILVERTON : What – what's this?

> [*The woman raises her own veil with her free hand*]

You!

WOMAN : Ah! Then you remember me?

MILVERTON [*flustered, but recovering his composure*] : But – but of course, dear lady! Forgive me! That veil – I confess . . .

WOMAN : A very good attempt, Mr. Milverton. But then, how could you forget me?

MILVERTON [*tittering nervously*] : No, no! Of course!

WOMAN : You have rather special reasons for remembering me, after all.

MILVERTON : A modest financial transaction. Purely in the way of business.

WOMAN [*hardening*] : Modest, did you say?

MILVERTON [*his habitual manner returning*] : Come, now, madam! I ask you, why was I driven to such extremities in your case? Why, your own obstinacy! I assure you, I did my best to accommodate you. My very best. But every man must, in the end, conduct his business how he can.

WOMAN : Business!

MILVERTON : I put my price well within your means. By turning your diamonds into paste you could have met it

easily. But no – you would be obstinate. You would not pay. I ask you, what was I to do?

WOMAN: You have killed my husband by sending those letters to him.

MILVERTON: *I* killed . . .? Oh, now . . .

WOMAN: I admit I was not fit to lace his boots for him. All the same, I humbled myself before you. I begged and prayed for your mercy. You laughed in my face – just as you're trying to laugh now.

MILVERTON [*laughs nervously*]: Dear lady . . .

WOMAN: So, Charles Augustus Milverton – what have you to say to me now?

MILVERTON [*a desperate bluff*]: Say? Why, only that if I were to raise my voice my servants would be here within a moment, and I could have you arrested for breaking into my house with a weapon. But never fear. I will make allowance for your natural anger. Leave the house at once, and nothing more need be said.

WOMAN: Oh no, Milverton. It will not be so easy as that. I came here to make sure that you will ruin no more lives as you ruined mine. I came to free the world of a poisonous thing.

[*She levels the revolver*]

MILVERTON [*holding up his hands as if to protect himself*]: No!

WOMAN: Yes, Milverton!

[*She fires. He falls forward with a cry. She fires two more shots into him as he lies before her. She looks down at him in momentary satisfaction, then, thrusting the revolver into her handbag and pulling down her veil, she glances round, sees the french window, goes swiftly to it and out.* HOLMES *and* WATSON *immediately emerge from round the sides of the curtains*]

WATSON: Great heavens! Should I have grabbed her, Holmes?

HOLMES: Let her go. Quickly, Watson – the rest of the letters. We haven't a moment to lose.

> [HOLMES *hurries to the safe, tears it open and stuffs the remaining letters into his bag, while* WATSON *stoops over* MILVERTON, *turns him slightly, then lets him fall back lifeless*]

WATSON: He's dead, all right.

> [*He listens*]

Holmes! Someone's coming!

> [HOLMES *is finishing his task. A girl's running footsteps are heard approaching along a passage*]

HOLMES: Your mask, Watson!

> [*They hastily readjust their masks.* HOLMES *rises. The door bursts open, revealing* AGATHA *She screams.* HOLMES *makes for the windows followed by* WATSON, *who trips over a rug* AGATHA *darts forward, catching him by the tai of his coat as he lumbers to his feet, but he jerks him self free and disappears after* HOLMES. AGATHA *stands there, dramatically pointing after them*]

AGATHA: Stop them! Murderers! Murderers!

> [*Quick curtain*]

SCENE FOUR

[*A drop representing two or three shop fronts in Regent Street. The one just to right of centre is a photographer's. A number of portraits are displayed, with, prominent amongst them, one of a woman in a 'Society Beauty' pose. A number of shoppers passing by and, perhaps, some recorded horse traffic effects could be used to advantage to establish the setting, but should not be allowed to distract attention from the main action.*

HOLMES *and* WATSON, *dressed in frock coats and tall hats, walk in from left, glancing at the shop windows. They do not quite reach the photographer's before* LESTRADE *enters from left hurrying after them*]

LESTRADE [*a little out of breath*] : Mr. Holmes! Mr. Holmes!

[HOLMES *and* WATSON *stop and look round*]

WATSON : Inspector Lestrade!

[LESTRADE *comes up*]

LESTRADE : Caught you up at last! Just missed you at Baker Street, but Mrs. Hudson said something about a stroll down Regent Street.

HOLMES : Quite correctly, as you see, Lestrade. But what brings you after us?

LESTRADE : You very busy, Mr. Holmes?

HOLMES [*guardedly*] : Not exactly. Scotland Yard in difficulties again?

LESTRADE : Well, I just thought, if you'd nothing particular on hand, you might care to assist us. Remarkable business last night at Hampstead.

[HOLMES *and* WATSON *cannot resist exchanging a swift glance*]

HOLMES: Dear me! What was it?

LESTRADE: Murder. Dramatic sort of affair. Fellow by name of Milverton.

HOLMES: Who? The murderer?

LESTRADE: No, no. He was the one done in. Mind you, we've had our eye on him for some time. Suspected of holding papers used for blackmailing.

HOLMES: Really?

LESTRADE: Yes. Well, he was shot dead last night at his house. Safe rifled.

WATSON: Burglar, you think?

LESTRADE: Don't reckon so. Some banknotes left there untouched, and a desk drawer full of them. No, you ask me, someone was after those papers of his. Couple of gents of position, most likely.

HOLMES: Oh, then it was murderers in the plural?

LESTRADE: Definitely. The first was a bit too active. Out of the french windows as quick as you'd say knife, according to the maid. The second wasn't so quick off the mark. The maid grabbed him, but he knocked her down and broke free. Plucky little girl, that.

[WATSON *looks down at his feet to hide a smile*]

HOLMES: Any description of – the second man?

LESTRADE: Middle-sized, strongly built – you know, square jaw, thick neck, moustache, mask over his eyes.

[WATSON *looks even harder at his boots*]

HOLMES: Hm! Rather vague. Why, it might be a description of Dr. Watson.

LESTRADE [*laughs heartily*]: Well now – that'd be a thing, Doctor, eh?

[WATSON *finds some difficulty in sharing the joke*]

HOLMES: So Milverton's dead, Lestrade! Well, well! I knew something of him. One of the most dangerous men in London, I often thought.

LESTRADE: You'll help us investigate it, Mr. Holmes?

HOLMES: You know, it's my view that there are certain crimes which the law cannot touch, and which, therefore, justify a measure of private revenge.

LESTRADE: Yes, but murder . . .

HOLMES: You're quite right, of course. Murder must be punished. But I have made up my mind, Lestrade. For once, my sympathies are with the criminals, rather than with the victim. No, I will not handle the case.

LESTRADE: Well! You disappoint me, Mr. Holmes. I should have thought this was just the sort of thing would have interested you.

HOLMES: Oh, it did – er – does. But I can see that, as usual, your superlative instincts are leading you precisely on the track of the two men you want. You'll distinguish yourself in your – ah – usual way without help from me.

LESTRADE [*puffing himself up a little*]: Ah, yes, it's very good of you to say that, Mr. Holmes. Still, I can flatter myself you're right. We have their descriptions, we have their footprints in the garden. If they were to walk past us here now I reckon I'd recognize them quick enough from what we've got.

[HOLMES *and* WATSON *again exchange glances*]

HOLMES: Capital!

LESTRADE: Yes, it's ten to one we trace them. Well, then, I'd better be getting on to the Yard. Nippy this morning. Quite a frost last night.

HOLMES: There was.

LESTRADE: Soon be Christmas. Good-day to you, gentlemen.

WATSON [*with some relief*] : Good day!

HOLMES : Good day, Lestrade!

> [*A mutual raising of hats as* LESTRADE *goes past them and exits right.* WATSON *takes off his hat and mops his brow with his handkerchief*]

WATSON : Oh, Holmes!

> [HOLMES *is greatly enjoying the situation*]

HOLMES [*laughing*] : My *dear* Watson!

WATSON : You sailed pretty close to the wind, didn't you?

HOLMES : No danger at all. Something tells me, Watson, there's going to be another unclosed file lying on Lestrade's desk for a long time to come.

WATSON [*fervently*] : I hope you're right!

HOLMES : Meanwhile, let us resume our stroll.

> [*They begin to walk towards right, but immediately halt at the photographer's window*]

But here we are, at our destination already!

WATSON : A photographer's! What for, Holmes?

HOLMES : The contemplation of Nature's skilful handiwork. Look!

> [*He points to the portrait of the woman*]

WATSON [*whistles*] : Holmes! It's her – from last night!

HOLMES : Exactly. I thought at the time I'd seen her somewhere recently. Only at breakfast this morning I recalled this shop window. And to think, Watson, that Lestrade stood just there, with all three persons involved within his sight! I fear I shall never have the satisfaction of telling him!

> [WATSON *has been peering more closely at the portrait*]

WATSON : Look, Holmes! It's got her title printed underneath!

> [*He straightens up*]

She's . . .

[HOLMES *swiftly raises his finger to his lips*]

HOLMES: SSH!

WATSON: Eh?

[HOLMES *leads* WATSON *slowly away towards right*]

HOLMES: No, my dear Watson. Don't speak it. Now that I have satisfied my curiosity, let us endeavour to put the noble lady's name out of our minds by talking of other things, while we resume our walk in this delightful winter sunshine.

[WATSON *nods vigorously as they exit, smiling, right, and the curtain falls*]

THE MAZARIN STONE

The setting is the parlour of 221B Baker Street, *evening*

Characters, in order of appearance:

BILLY: Holmes's page-boy. 'The young, but very wise and tactful page . . .'

DR. WATSON: (Now married and living elsewhere).

SHERLOCK HOLMES

MRS. HUDSON

COUNT NEGRETTO SYLVIUS: Big-game hunter, sportsman, card-player and man-about-town. Half Italian; suave, dangerous, and in early middle-age.

SAM MERTON: A punch-drunk boxer. 'A large and ugly gentleman.'

A POLICE SERGEANT AND TWO CONSTABLES

LORD CANTLEMERE: A supercilious, elderly peer of high standing. 'A thin, austere figure with a hatchet face and drooping mid-Victorian whiskers . . .'

F

THE MAZARIN STONE

[*The parlour of* 221B *Baker Street. For this play,
whose entire action takes place here, a curtain at the
back of the stage must be capable of being drawn
aside to reveal an alcove, backed by a window with
blinds drawn. Seated beside this window, in profile
to it and to the audience, is a dummy representing
Sherlock Holmes. It is wearing an old dressing-
gown, and sits in a large, high-backed chair. If the
window-blind were not down, it would appear to
occupants of the houses opposite that* HOLMES *himself is seated there. When the play begins, the chair
and its occupant are concealed from the audience
by the alcove curtain.*

*Two doorways are necessary: one for characters
arriving and departing – 'parlour door' – and one
leading off into* HOLMES'S *bedroom – 'bedroom
door'. As the course of the action will reveal, an off-
stage route is necessary between the 'bedroom' and
the alcove.*

The lamp is lit. A parasol stands against a chair.
BILLY, *the page-boy, is holding up* HOLMES'S
ulster, brushing it vigorously.
There is a tap at the parlour door. It opens, and
WATSON'S *head peers round*]

BILLY: Dr. Watson, sir! Come in, sir!

[WATSON *enters, closing the door*]

WATSON: Well, Billy, my boy! Keeping the moths at bay?

BILLY: That's it, sir.

> [*He folds the coat and puts it down on a chair, as* WATSON *lays aside his hat and stick.* WATSON *glances round the room*]

WATSON: It doesn't seem to have changed much, Billy.

BILLY: Not much, sir.

WATSON: You don't change, either. I hope the same can be said of *him*?

BILLY: I think he's in bed and asleep.

WATSON [*laughs*]: At seven o'clock of a lovely summer's evening. He *hasn't* changed, then! I suppose it means a case?

BILLY: Yes, sir. He's very hard at it just now. Fair frightens me.

WATSON: What does?

BILLY: His health, Dr. Watson. He gets paler, and thinner, and he never eats nothing. I heard Mrs. Hudson asking him when he would take his dinner. 'Seven-thirty,' he told her – '*the day after tomorrow!*'

WATSON [*sighs*]: Yes, Billy, I know how it is.

BILLY [*confidentially*]: I can tell you one thing, sir – he's following somebody.

> [WATSON, *amused, copies* BILLY'S *manner and leans towards him conspiratorially*]

WATSON: Really?

BILLY: One disguise after another. Yesterday he was a workman, looking for a job. Today he was an old woman. Fairly took me in, he did – and I ought to know his ways by now.

> [*He picks up the parasol briefly*]

Part of the old girl's outfit.

WATSON [*laughs*]: What's it all about, Billy?

BILLY [*glancing round cautiously*] : I don't mind telling *you*, sir – but it shouldn't go no farther . . .

> [WATSON *gives his head a meaningful shake and places a finger to his lips*]

It's this case of the Crown Diamond.

WATSON : What – the hundred-thousand-pound burglary?

BILLY : Yes, sir. They must get it back. Why, we've had the Prime Minister and Home Secretary both sat in this very room!

WATSON : You don't say!

BILLY : Mr. Holmes was very nice to them. Promised he would do all he could. Then there's Lord Cantlemere.

WATSON [*dismally*] : Oh!

BILLY : Ah, you know what that means, Dr. Watson! He's a stiff 'un, and no mistake. Now, I can get along with the Prime Minister – and I've nothing against the Home Secretary . . . But I can't *stand* his lordship!

WATSON [*laughs heartily*].

BILLY : Mr. Holmes can't, neither, sir! You can tell, Lord Cantlemere don't believe in Mr. Holmes. He was against employing him, and he'd rather he failed.

WATSON : And Mr. Holmes knows it?

BILLY : Mr. Holmes *always* knows what there is to know.

WATSON [*hastily*] : Oh, quite, quite! Well, Billy, we'll just hope that he won't fail, and then Lord Cantlemere will be confounded. But I'd better be getting home to my wife.

> [*He moves towards his hat and stick, but catches sight of the curtain*]

I say, Billy! Bit early to have the curtains drawn and the lamp lit, isn't it?

BILLY : Well – there's something funny behind there.

WATSON: Something *funny*?

BILLY: You can see it, sir.

> [BILLY *draws the curtain, revealing the dummy*]

WATSON: Bless my soul!

BILLY: Yes, sir.

WATSON [*examining the figure*]: A perfect replica of Sherlock Holmes! Dressing-gown and all!

> [BILLY *turns the chair so that the dummy chances to finish up with its back to the parlour door*]

BILLY: We put it at different angles every now and then, like this, so's it'll look more lifelike. Mind, I wouldn't dare touch it if the blind wasn't drawn. When it's up you can see this from right across the way.

WATSON: We used something of the sort once before, you know.

BILLY: Before my time, sir.

WATSON: Er – yes.

> [*Unseen by either of them the bedroom door opens and* HOLMES *appears in his dressing-gown*]

BILLY: There's folk who watch us from over yonder, sir. You may catch a peep of them now.

> [*He is about to pull back a corner of the blind to enable* WATSON *to look out*]

HOLMES [*sharply*]: That will do, Billy!

> [BILLY *and* WATSON *spin round*]

WATSON: Holmes!

HOLMES [*severely*]: You were in danger of your life, then, my boy. I can't do without you just yet.

BILLY [*humbly*]: Yes, sir.

HOLMES: That will be all for now.

BILLY: Very good, sir.

> [*He exits by the parlour door*]

HOLMES: That boy is a problem, Watson. How far am I justified in letting him be in danger?

WATSON: Danger of what, Holmes?

HOLMES: Of sudden death.

WATSON: Holmes!

HOLMES: But it's good to see you in your old quarters once again, my dear Watson!

WATSON [*concerned*]: Holmes – this talk of sudden death. What are you expecting?

HOLMES [*simply*]: To be murdered.

WATSON: Oh, come now! You're joking!

HOLMES: Even my limited sense of humour could evolve a better joke than that, Watson. [*Brightening*] But we may be comfortable in the meantime, mayn't we? Is alcohol permitted? The gasogene and cigars are in the old place.

[They bustle about accordingly]

Let me see you once more in the customary chair.

WATSON: Pleasure, Holmes!

HOLMES: I hope you haven't learned to despise my pipe and my lamentable tobacco? It has to take the place of food these days.

[He sinks into his chair and proceeds to light up, as WATSON *finishes pouring and hands him a drink]*

WATSON: But why not eat?

HOLMES: Because the faculties become refined when you starve them. Surely, as a doctor, you must admit that what your digestion gains in the way of blood supply is so much lost to the brain? *I* am a brain, Watson. The rest of me is mere appendix. Therefore, it's the brain I must consider.

WATSON [*sitting down*]: Well, good health, anyway, Holmes.

HOLMES: And to you, my dear fellow!

[They drink]

WATSON: But – this danger . . .?

HOLMES: Ah, yes. Just in case it should come off it would be as well for you to know the name of the murderer. You can give it to Scotland Yard, with my love and a parting blessing.

WATSON: Holmes!

HOLMES: His name is Sylvius – Count Negretto Sylvius, No. 136, Moorside Gardens, London N.W. Got it?

WATSON: Yes. [*Hesitantly*]: Er – Holmes . . . I've got nothing to do for a day or two. Count me in.

HOLMES [*sadly shaking his head*]: Your morals don't improve, Watson.

WATSON: My *morals*?

HOLMES: You've added fibbing to your other vices. You bear every sign of the busy medical man, with calls on him every hour.

WATSON: Not such important ones. But – can't you have this fellow arrested?

HOLMES: Yes, Watson, I could. That's what worries him so.

WATSON: Then why don't you?

HOLMES: Because I don't know where the diamond is.

WATSON: Ah! Billy was telling me – the missing Crown Jewel!

HOLMES: The great yellow Mazarin Stone. I've cast my net and I have my fish. But I have *not* got the stone. Yes, I could make the world a better place by laying *them* by the heels; but it's the stone I want.

WATSON: And is Count Sylvius one of your fish?

HOLMES: Yes – and he's a *shark*. He bites. The other is Sam Merton, the boxer. Not a bad fellow, Sam, but the Count has used him. Sam's just a great, big, silly, bull-headed

gudgeon; but he's flopping about in my net, all the same.

WATSON: Where is Count Sylvius now?

HOLMES: I've been at his elbow all morning.

[*He gets up*]

You've seen me as an old lady, Watson?

WATSON [*chuckling*]: Oh, yes indeed!

[HOLMES *assumes the posture and walk of an old lady*]

[*In a cracked old voice*]: I was never more convincing, Doctor. Never!

[WATSON *laughs as* HOLMES *straightens up*]

[*Normal voice*]: He actually picked up my parasol for me once.

[HOLMES *picks up the parasol and gesticulates with it*]

WATSON: He didn't!

[HOLMES *makes an elaborate bow, holding out the parasol in both hands*]

HOLMES [*mimicking Sylvius*]: By your leave, madame.

[HOLMES *resumes his normal voice and manner and lays the parasol aside*]

He's half Italian, you know. Full of the Southern graces when he's in the mood. But he's a devil incarnate in the other mood. Life is full of whimsical happenings, Watson.

WATSON [*with a snort*]: Whimsical! It might have been tragedy!

HOLMES: Well, perhaps it might. Anyway, I followed him to old Straubenzee's workshop in the Minories. Straubenzee made the air-gun – a very pretty bit of work, as I understand. I fancy it's in the opposite window at present, ready to put a bullet through this dummy's beautiful head whenever I choose to raise that blind.

[*Knock at parlour door, which opens.* BILLY *enters, carrying a salver*]

BILLY: Mr. Holmes, sir . . .

HOLMES: What is it, Billy?

BILLY: There's a gentleman to see you, sir.

[HOLMES *takes the visiting card from the salver and looks at it*]

HOLMES: Thank you.

[*He replaces the card*]

The man himself, Watson!

WATSON: Sylvius!

HOLMES [*nods*]: I'd hardly expected this. Grasp the nettle, eh! A man of nerve, Watson. But possibly you've heard of his reputation as a big-game shooter? It'd be a triumphant ending to his excellent sporting record if he added me to his bag.

WATSON: Send for the police, Holmes!

HOLMES: I probably shall – but not just yet. Would you just glance carefully out of the window and see if anyone is hanging about in the street?

WATSON: Certainly.

[*He goes to the window and peeps cautiously round the corner of the blind*]

Yes – there's a rough-looking fellow near the door.

HOLMES: That will be Sam Merton – the faithful but rather fatuous Sam. Billy, where is Count Sylvius?

BILLY: In the waiting-room, sir.

HOLMES: Show him up when I ring.

BILLY: Yes, sir.

HOLMES: If I'm not in the room, show him in all the same.

BILLY: Very good, Mr. Holmes.

[*He leaves by the parlour door*]

WATSON: Look here, Holmes, this is simply ridiculous. This is a desperate man who sticks at nothing, you'd have me believe. He may have *come* to murder you.

HOLMES: I shouldn't be surprised.

WATSON: Then I insist on staying with you!

HOLMES: You'd be horribly in the way.

WATSON: In *his* way!

HOLMES: No, my dear fellow – in mine.

[WATSON *sits down stubbornly*]

WATSON: Be that as it may, I can't possibly leave you.

HOLMES: Yes you can, Watson. And you will – for you've never failed to play the game. I'm sure you'll play it to the end.

[*He crosses to his desk and begins to scribble a note*]

This man has come for his own purpose, but he may stay for mine. I want you to take a cab to Scotland Yard and give this note to Youghal, of the C.I.D. Come back with the police.

WATSON [*rising*]: I'll do that with joy!

HOLMES [*handing Watson the note*]: Before you get back I may just have time to find out where the stone is. Now, I'll just ring for Billy to show him up, and I think we'll go out through the bedroom.

[HOLMES *presses a bell, while* WATSON *gathers his things.* HOLMES *ushers him towards the bedroom door*]

This second exit is exceedingly useful, you know. I rather want to see my shark without his seeing me.

[WATSON *halts*]

WATSON: The dummy! Shouldn't the curtain be drawn over it again?

HOLMES: No, no. We'll leave it as it is.

[*He moves swiftly to the dummy*]

Perhaps just a touch to this noble head . . .

[*He adjusts the head to bow upon the breast*]

As though somewhere in the middle of forty winks.

[*He ensures that the dummy has its back to the parlour door*]

There! Now, come along.

WATSON: I hope you know what you're doing, that's all!

[*They exit by the bedroom door, closing it behind them. A slight pause, then the parlour door opens.* BILLY *enters and* COUNT SYLVIUS *walks in past him*]

BILLY: If you'll just wait, sir.

[SYLVIUS *ignores him.* BILLY *withdraws, closing the door behind him.* SYLVIUS *looks round the room for a moment, then notices the dummy. He grips his stick more firmly and creeps a cautious pace or two towards it. Satisfied that the figure is dozing, he steps forward and raises his stick to strike.* HOLMES *enters silently from the bedroom*]

HOLMES: Don't break it, Count Sylvius!

[SYLVIUS *whirls round, his stick still upraised, a look of disbelief on his face*]

SYLVIUS: What!

HOLMES: It's a pretty little thing.

[SYLVIUS *lowers the stick and walks round to look at the dummy in astonishment*]

Tavernier, the French modeller, made it. He's as good at waxworks as your friend Straubenzee is at air-guns.

[HOLMES *turns the chair to face the window. The dummy is now completely hidden from the audience*]

SYLVIUS: Air-guns? What do you mean, sir?

HOLMES: Put your stick on the side-table, before you're tempted to do any other form of damage.

[*There is a momentary hesitation, in which we think* SYLVIUS *might spring at* HOLMES. *But* HOLMES *stands still, looking at him hard, one hand in his pocket, in which we sense him to have a revolver.* SYLVIUS *relaxes and obeys*]

SYLVIUS: Very well.

HOLMES: Thank you. Would you care to put your revolver out, also?

[*At the mention of revolver* SYLVIUS'*s hand flies to his hip pocket. He does not draw, but stands poised defiantly*]

[*Blandly*]: Oh, very well, if you prefer to sit on it.

[HOLMES *moves to a chair and sits*]

Your visit is really most opportune, Count Sylvius. I wanted badly to have a few minutes' chat with you.

[SYLVIUS *stumps over to a chair opposite* HOLMES]

SYLVIUS: I, too, wished to have some words with you, Holmes! That is why I am here. Because you have gone out of your way to annoy me. Because you have put your creatures on my track!

HOLMES: Oh, I assure you no!

SYLVIUS: I have had them followed! Two can play at that game, Holmes!

HOLMES: It's a small point, Count Sylvius, but perhaps you would kindly give me my prefix when you address me? You can understand that, with my routine of work, I should find myself on familiar terms with half the rogues' gallery, and you'll agree that exceptions are invidious.

SYLVIUS [*sneering*]: Well, *Mr.* Holmes, then.

HOLMES: That's better. But I assure you that you're mistaken about my alleged agents.

SYLVIUS [*laughs contemptuously*]: Other people can observe as

well as you! Yesterday there was an old sporting man. Today it was an elderly woman. They kept me in view all day.

HOLMES: Really, sir, you compliment me! Old Baron Dowson said the night before he was hanged that in my case what the law had gained the stage had lost.

SYLVIUS: It . . . It was you?

HOLMES: You can see in the corner the parasol which you so politely handed to me in the Minories before you began to suspect.

SYLVIUS: If I had known that, you might never have . . .

HOLMES: . . . have seen this humble abode again? I was well aware of that. But, as it happens, you did *not* know, so here we are!

SYLVIUS: So it was not your agents, but your play-acting, busybodying self! You admit that you dogged me. Why?

HOLMES: Come now, Count: you used to shoot lions in Algeria.

SYLVIUS: What about it?

HOLMES: Why did you?

SYLVIUS: The sport – the excitement – the danger.

HOLMES: And, no doubt, to free the country from a pest?

SYLVIUS: Exactly.

HOLMES: My reasons in a nutshell!

[SYLVIUS *springs to his feet in fury and reaches instinctively towards his revolver pocket*]

SYLVIUS: For that, I will . . .!

HOLMES: Sit down, sir, sit down!

[*He gives* SYLVIUS *a steely stare.* SYLVIUS *hesitates for a moment, then obeys*]

I had another, more practical reason for following your movements. I want that yellow diamond.

[SYLVIUS *begins to relax and chuckle. He stretches his legs and makes himself comfortable*]

SYLVIUS: Upon my word – *Mr.* Holmes!

HOLMES: You know that I was after you for that. The real reason why you're here tonight is to find out how much I know and how far my removal is absolutely essential. Well, I should say that from *your* point of view it *is* absolutely essential. You see, I know all about the diamond – save only one thing, which you are about to tell me.

SYLVIUS: Indeed? Pray, what is this missing fact?

HOLMES: Where the Crown diamond now is.

SYLVIUS: And how should I be able to tell you that?

HOLMES: You can, and you will.

SYLVIUS: You astonish me!

HOLMES: You can't bluff me, Count Sylvius. You are absolute plate-glass. I can see to the very back of your mind.

SYLVIUS: Oh! Then, of course, you can see where the diamond is.

HOLMES [*delighted*]: Then you *do* know!

SYLVIUS: No!

HOLMES: You've admitted it.

SYLVIUS: I admit nothing!

[HOLMES *gets up and goes to a drawer, which he opens*]

HOLMES: Now, Count, if you'll be reasonable we can do business.

SYLVIUS: And *you* talk about bluff!

[HOLMES *takes a notebook from the drawer*]

HOLMES: Do you know what I keep in this book?

SYLVIUS: No, sir. I do not.

HOLMES: I keep *you* in it.

SYLVIUS: Me?

HOLMES: You are all here – every action of your vile and dangerous life.

SYLVIUS: There are limits to my patience, Holmes!

HOLMES [*waving the book at Sylvius*]: Yes, it's all here: the real facts about the death of old Mrs. Harold, who left you the Blymer estate to gamble away.

> [HOLMES *taunts* SYLVIUS *with the book,* SYLVIUS *making a grab for it whenever it approaches, but always missing*]

SYLVIUS: You're dreaming!

HOLMES: And the complete life history of Miss Minnie Warrender.

SYLVIUS: You'll make nothing of that!

HOLMES: There's plenty more, Count: the robbery in the train-de-luxe to the Riviera on February 13th, 1892; the forged cheque in the same year on the Credit Lyonnais.

SYLVIUS: No! There you *are* mistaken!

HOLMES: Then I *am* right on the others!

> [*He throws the book into the drawer, which he closes, resuming his seat*]

Now, Count, you're a card-player. You know that when the other fellow has all the trumps it saves time to throw in your hand.

SYLVIUS: Just what has all this talk to do with the jewel?

HOLMES: Gently, Count! Restrain that eager mind! Let me get to the points in my own humdrum fashion.

> [*Gesturing towards the closed drawer*]

I have all that against you. But, above all, I have a clear case against you and your fighting bully in the theft of the Crown diamond.

SYLVIUS: Indeed?

HOLMES [*enumerating the points on his fingers*] : I have the cabman who took you to Whitehall, and the cabman who brought you away. I have the commissionaire who saw you near the case. I have Ikey Sanders, who refused to cut the stone up for you. Ikey has talked, Count, and the game is up!

SYLVIUS: I don't believe you!

HOLMES: That's the hand I play from. I put it all on the table. Only one card is missing. It's the King of Diamonds. I don't know where the stone is.

[*He presses the bell*]

SYLVIUS: And you never will! Why are you ringing that bell?

[*He gets to his feet suspiciously*]

HOLMES: Be reasonable, Count! Consider the situation. You are going to be locked up for twenty years. So is Sam Merton. What good are you going to get out of your diamond? None in the world. But if you hand it over – well, I'm prepared to compound a felony. We don't want you or Sam. We want the stone. Give that up, Count Sylvius, and so far as I'm concerned you can go free. But if you make another slip in the future . . .! Well, it'll be the last.

SYLVIUS: And if I refuse?

HOLMES [*sighs*] : Then I'm afraid it must be you, and not the stone.

[*Knock at parlour door.* BILLY *enters*]

BILLY: Did you ring, sir?

HOLMES: Yes, Billy. You will see a large and ugly gentleman outside the front door. Ask him to come up.

BILLY: Yes, sir.

[*He is about to go, but hesitates*]

G

What if he won't, sir?

HOLMES: Oh, no violence, Billy! Don't be rough with him!
If you tell him that Count Sylvius wants him he will
come.

BILLY: Very good, sir.

[*He exits with a grin, closing the door*]

HOLMES: I think it would be as well to have your friend Sam
at this conference. After all, his interests should be repre-
sented.

[SYLVIUS *resumes his seat*]

SYLVIUS: Just what do you intend to do now?

HOLMES: I was remarking to my friend, Dr. Watson, a short
while ago that I had a shark and a gudgeon in my net.
Now I'm drawing in the net, and up they come together.

SYLVIUS: You won't die in your bed, Holmes!

HOLMES: I've often had that same idea. But does it matter
very much? After all, Count, you own exit is more likely
to be perpendicular than horizontal.

[SYLVIUS'S *hand jerks towards his gun-pocket.*
HOLMES *waves an admonishing finger*]

HOLMES: It's no use, my friend. Even if I gave you time to
draw it, you know perfectly well you daren't use it.
Nasty, noisy things, revolvers. Better stick to air-guns.

[*Knock at parlour door.* BILLY *shows in* SAM
MERTON *coldly and withdraws without speaking.*
MERTON *glares about him, tensed for action*]

Good day, Mr. Merton. Rather dull in the street, isn't
it?

MERTON: What's up, Count?

HOLMES: If I may put it in a nutshell, Mr. Merton, I should
say the *game* was up.

MERTON: 'Ere! Is this cove trying to be funny? I'm not in the
funny mood meself.

HOLMES: I think I can promise you'll feel even less humorous as the evening advances.

[MERTON *lumbers aggressively towards* HOLMES, *but is halted by a gesture from* SYLVIUS]

SYLVIUS: That will do, Sam!

HOLMES: Thank you, Count.

[HOLMES *gets to his feet*]

Now, look here – I'm a busy man and I can't waste time. I'm going into that bedroom to try over the Hoffman Barcarolle on my violin. You can explain to your friend how the matter lies, without the restraint of my presence.

[HOLMES *goes to the bedroom door*]

In five minutes I shall return for your final answer. You quite grasp the alternative, don't you? Shall we take you, or shall we have the stone?

[HOLMES *exits, closing the bedroom door behind him.* SYLVIUS *jumps up and paces about thoughtfully*]

MERTON: 'Offman who? What's the chap on about?

SYLVIUS: Shut up, Sam! Let me think!

[*Sounds of violin strings being plucked and tuned in the bedroom*]

MERTON: If it's trouble, why didn't you plug 'im?

SYLVIUS: You're a fool, Sam! Anyone but you could have seen he was holding a revolver in his dressing-gown pocket.

MERTON: Aw!

[*The violin begins to play the Barcarolle from* 'The Tales of Hoffman'. *It is expertly played. Having established it, diminish somewhat under following dialogue*]

MERTON [*disgustedly*]: Cor!

SYLVIUS: Ikey Sanders has split on us.

MERTON: Split, 'as 'e? I'll do 'im a thick 'un for that, if I swing for it!

SYLVIUS: How do you think that will help us? We've got to make up our minds what to do.

MERTON [*lowering his voice*]: 'Arf a mo', Count! That's a leary cove in there. D'you suppose 'e's listening?

SYLVIUS: How can he listen and play that thing?

MERTON: Aw, that's right!

SYLVIUS: Now *you* listen! He can lag us over this stone, but he's offered to let us slip if we only tell him where it is.

MERTON: Wot! Give up a 'undred thousand quid!

SYLVIUS: It's one or the other. He knows too much.

MERTON: Well . . . listen! 'E's alone in there. Let's do 'im! Then we've nothing to fear of.

SYLVIUS: He's armed and ready. If we shot him we could hardly get away in a place like this. Besides, it's likely enough the police know he's on to something. Listen!

[*They listen. The violin plays steadily on*]

It was just a noise in the street, I think.

MERTON: Look, guv'nor – you've got the brains. If slugging's no use, then it's up to you.

SYLVIUS: I've fooled better men than Holmes. The stone's here, in my secret pocket. I take no chances leaving it about. It can be out of England tonight and cut into four pieces in Amsterdam before Sunday. One of us must slip round to Lime Street with the stone and tell Van Seddar to get off by the next boat.

MERTON: But the false bottom ain't ready yet. Van Seddar don't expect to go till next week!

SYLVIUS: He must go now, and chance it. As to Holmes, we can fool him. We'll promise him the stone, then put him

on the wrong track; and by the time he finds out we'll be in Holland, too.

MERTON: Now you're talking, Count!

SYLVIUS: You go now and see the Dutchman, Sam. Here . . .

[SYLVIUS *pulls* SAM *aside*]

Just in case, come out of line with that keyhole.

[SYLVIUS *reaches into his secret pocket and produces a large yellow gem. The 'dummy' in the chair near the window begins to move cautiously, and we see that during the preceding dialogue* HOLMES *has contrived to seat himself in its place. Unobserved by* SYLVIUS *or* MERTON *he sidles towards them. He has a revolver in his hand*]

MERTON: I don't know 'ow you dare carry it about!

SYLVIUS: Where could I keep it safer? If we could take it out of Whitehall, someone else could easily take it from my lodgings.

[HOLMES *sneaks quickly forward and plucks the stone from* SYLVIUS'S *hand*]

HOLMES: Or out of your hand!

[SYLVIUS *and* MERTON *are too flabbergasted to react. They stare speechlessly at* HOLMES, *and then at the chair*]

Thank you, Count. It will be safe with me.

MERTON: There was a blooming waxworks in that chair!

[*He jerks the chair round; it is empty.* HOLMES *moves carefully back to a position from where he can cover them both*]

HOLMES: Your surprise is very natural, Mr. Merton. You are not aware, of course, that a second door from my bedroom leads behind that curtain. I fancied you must have heard me, Count, as I slipped into the dummy's chair, but luck and a passing cab were on my side. They

enabled me to listen to your racy conversation, which would have been painfully constrained had you been aware of my presence.

[SYLVIUS *lurches towards* HOLMES, *who raises the revolver slightly*]

SYLVIUS: Deuce take you, Holmes!

HOLMES: No violence, gentlemen! Consider the furniture!

[*They stand still*]

It must be very clear to you that the position is an impossible one. The police are waiting below.

MERTON: Guv'nor? Shall I . . .?

SYLVIUS [*resignedly*]: No, Sam. I give you best, Holmes. I believe you are the devil himself.

HOLMES: Not *far* from him, at any rate.

[MERTON *suddenly points to the bedroom door*]

MERTON: 'Ere! That blooming fiddle! It's playing itself!

HOLMES: Oh, let it play. These modern gramophones are a remarkable invention!

MERTON: Aw!

[*Men's voices approaching the parlour door. It opens suddenly.* WATSON *hastens in*]

WATSON: This way, officers!

[*A police sergeant and two constables hurry after him and seize* SYLVIUS *and* MERTON]

SERGEANT: Come on, Sam! We've been waiting to get hold of you!

MERTON: Gar!

SYLVIUS: Take your hands off me, my man!

CONSTABLE: Not blooming likely!

[*They are led away, struggling. At the door,* MERTON *stops, looks back into the room, then at* HOLMES]

MERTON: Waxworks! Grammerphones! Garrr!

[*He is led off as* BILLY *enters*]

BILLY [*with distaste*]: Lord Cantlemere is here, sir.

[HOLMES *goes to the bedroom door*]

HOLMES: Show his lordship up, Billy, while I turn off the –
er – 'grammerphone'.

BILLY: Very good, sir.

[HOLMES *and* BILLY *exit by the bedroom and
parlour doors respectively, leaving both of them
open.* WATSON *lays down his hat and stick. The
music ceases abruptly and* HOLMES *returns,
shutting the bedroom door.* BILLY *re-enters the
parlour door*]

BILLY: Lord Cantlemere, sir.

[*He steps aside to let* CANTLEMERE *enter, then
goes out, closing the door*]

CANTLEMERE: What on earth's going on here, Holmes?
Constables and fellahs all over the place!

HOLMES: How do you do, Lord Cantlemere? May I intro-
duce my friend and colleague, Dr. Watson?

WATSON: How d'you do, my lord?

CANTLEMERE [*brusquely*]: D'yer do?

HOLMES: Watson, pray help me with his lordship's overcoat.

[HOLMES *takes hold of the coat, preparing to take
it off*]

CANTLEMERE: No, thank you. I will not take it off.

[HOLMES *pawing the coat*]

HOLMES: Oh, but my friend Dr. Watson would assure you
that it is most unhealthy to retain a coat indoors, even
at this time of the year.

CANTLEMERE [*releasing himself*]: I am quite comfortable as I

am, sir! I have no need to stay. I have simply looked in to know how your self-appointed task is progressing.

[HOLMES *assumes a troubled air*]

HOLMES: It's difficult – very difficult.

CANTLEMERE [*with gleeful malice*]: Ha! I feared you'd find it so! Every man finds his limitations, Holmes – but at least it cures us of the weakness of self-satisfaction.

HOLMES: Yes, sir. I admit I have been much perplexed.

CANTLEMERE: No doubt!

HOLMES: Especially upon one point. Perhaps you could help me?

[CANTLEMERE *takes a chair.* HOLMES *sits opposite him,* WATSON *standing behind his chair*]

CANTLEMERE: You apply for my advice rather late in the day. I thought you had your own self-sufficient methods. Still, I am ready to help you.

HOLMES: Your lordship is most obliging. You see, we can no doubt frame a case against the actual thieves.

CANTLEMERE: *When* you've caught them.

HOLMES: Exactly. But the question is – how shall we proceed against the receiver?

CANTLEMERE: Receiver? Isn't this rather premature?

HOLMES: It's as well to have our plans ready. Now, what would you regard as final evidence against the receiver?

CANTLEMERE: The actual possession of the stone, of course.

HOLMES: You'd arrest him on that?

CANTLEMERE: Undoubtedly.

HOLMES [*slyly*]: In that case, my dear sir, I shall be under the painful necessity of advising your arrest!

[CANTLEMERE *leaps to his feet*]

CANTLEMERE: Holmes! In fifty years of official life I cannot recall such a liberty being taken! I am a busy man, engaged upon important affairs, and I have neither time nor taste for foolish jokes.

[HOLMES *slowly rises*]

I may tell you frankly, sir, that I have never been a believer in your powers. I have always been of the opinion that the matter was far safer in the hands of the regular police force. Your conduct confirms all my conclusions.

[*He moves stiffly towards the parlour door*]

I have the honour, sir, to wish you good evening!

HOLMES: One moment, sir!

[CANTLEMERE *turns to face him inquiringly*]

Actually to go off with the Mazarin Stone would be an even more serious offence than to be found in temporary possession of it!

CANTLEMERE: Sir, this is intolerable!

HOLMES: Put your hand in the right-hand pocket of your overcoat.

CANTLEMERE: What? What do you mean?

HOLMES: Come, come! Do what I ask!

[CANTLEMERE *splutters with fury, but feels in his pocket*]

CANTLEMERE: I'll make an end to this charade, and you'll wish you'd never begun it! I . . . I . . .

[*His fury suddenly abates, giving way to surprise, then astonishment, as he slowly withdraws from his pocket the Mazarin Stone and holds it up*]

WATSON: Great heavens!

HOLMES: Too bad of me, Lord Cantlemere. My old friend here will tell you that I have an impish habit of practical

joking. Also that I can never resist a dramatic situation. I took the liberty – the very great liberty, I confess – of putting the stone into your pocket at the beginning of our interview.

CANTLEMERE: I . . . I'm bewildered! This *is* the Mazarin Stone!

[HOLMES *bows slightly*]

Hol . . . *Mr.* Holmes, we are greatly your debtors. Your sense of humour may, as you admit, be somewhat perverted, and its exhibition untimely – remarkably untimely!

[WATSON *stifles a grin*]

But at least I withdraw any reflection I have made upon your professional powers.

HOLMES: Thank you, Lord Cantlemere. I hope your pleasure in reporting this successful result in the exalted circle to which you return will be some small atonement for my joke. I will supply the full particulars in a written report.

[CANTLEMERE *bows and goes to the parlour door.* WATSON *hastens to open it for him*]

Once more, good evening.

[*He nods to* WATSON]

And to you, sir, good evening.

WATSON: ⎫
HOLMES: ⎭ Good evening.

[CANTLEMERE *exits.* WATSON *gives him a rigid military salute behind his retreating back, then closes the door*]

WATSON: *Well*, Holmes.

HOLMES: He's an excellent and loyal person, but rather of the old régime.

[*He goes to* WATSON *and claps him on the shoulder*]

And now, my dear Watson, pray touch the bell, and Mrs. Hudson shall lay dinner for two – as of old!

[*Final curtain*]

THE BLUE CARBUNCLE

Characters, in order of appearance:

SHERLOCK HOLMES

DR. WATSON

PETERSON: A commissionaire. 'A very honest fellow.' Middle-aged, bearded, with a military carriage.

BAKER: A scholar. Elderly, with an over-precise, scholarly mode of speech and uncared-for clothes. 'A touch of red in nose and cheeks, with a slight tremor of his extended hand, recalled Holmes's surmise as to his habits.' *N.B.* The hat which Holmes finds much too large for his own head must *fit* Baker!

WINDIGATE: Landlord of the Alpha Inn. 'The ruddy, white-aproned landlord.' Portly, beaming, middle-aged to elderly.

BRECKINRIDGE: A Covent Garden stallholder. 'When you see a man with whiskers of that cut and the *Pink 'Un* protruding out of his pocket, you can always draw him by a bet.'

Young to middle-aged; belligerent, scornful – the sort of man who will argue passionately about sport, but would never dream of taking up any game.

BILL: A glum lad of fourteen or so.

RYDER: Head attendant at the Cosmopolitan Hotel. Weedy, pale-faced, middle-aged. 'The little man stood glancing from one to the other of us with half-frightened, half-hopeful eyes, as one who is not sure whether he is on the verge of a windfall or of a catastrophe.'

Customers at the Alpha Inn, and shoppers in Covent Garden market.

THE BLUE CARBUNCLE

SCENE ONE

> [*The parlour of* 221B *Baker Street.* HOLMES *lounges in a dressing-gown on the sofa. On the back of a chair beside him hangs a nondescript billycock (or bowler) hat.* HOLMES *is regarding it through a large magnifying glass, held out at arm's length. There is a knock at the door*]

HOLMES: Come in!

> [WATSON *enters, wearing a heavy coat and carrying his hat and cane*]

HOLMES [*sitting up*]: My *dear* Watson!

WATSON: Holmes! The compliments of the season to you!

HOLMES: And to you, my dear fellow. Throw off your things and take a chair.

> [WATSON *takes off his coat and throws it and his other things across the table. He sits on the sofa at* HOLMES'S *feet*]

WATSON: Just thought I'd look in. You're busy, though?

HOLMES: No, no. Something perfectly trivial – though to tell you the truth it's not without interest.

WATSON: Another of those homely little matters that end in someone going down for seven years' hard, eh, Holmes?

HOLMES [*laughs*]: Not this time. Just one of those whimsical little incidents which will happen when you have four million beings all jostling each other within the space of a few square miles.

WATSON: Well, let's hear about it, then.

HOLMES: You know Peterson, the commissionaire at the Langham Hotel?

WATSON: Certainly. Good fellow.

HOLMES [*indicating the hat*]: Well, this trophy belongs to him.

[WATSON *regards the hat with distaste*]

WATSON: That hat!

HOLMES: Oh, my dear Watson, don't be so contemptuous of it, please. Look upon it, if you will, not as a battered billycock, but as an intellectual problem.

WATSON: All right, then. Trophy, you say? Where'd it come from?

HOLMES: It arrived here yesterday, on Christmas morning, in company with a fine, fat goose, which I've no doubt is roasting at this moment in front of Peterson's fire.

WATSON: Oh?

HOLMES: The facts are these. About four o'clock on Christmas morning, Peterson was on his way home from some small jollification, as he called it.

WATSON [*laughs*]

HOLMES: As he was walking down Tottenham Court Road he saw, in the gaslight, a tallish man, walking with a slight stagger, and carrying a goose slung over his shoulder. At the corner of Goodge Street the fellow ran into a group of roughs. One of them promptly knocked his hat off.

WATSON: Naturally!

HOLMES: The man raised his stick to defend himself, and in doing so smashed the shop window behind his back. Peterson rushed forward to help him. Oh, I should have told you that Peterson was still wearing his uniform. He'd been 'on his way home' since the night before.

WATSON [*laughs*]

HOLMES: Well, seeing an imposing figure like Peterson bearing down on him was too much for this poor fellow's nerve. He dropped the goose and took to his heels.

WATSON: Leaving his goose!

HOLMES: Yes. The roughs had made off, too. Peterson was left in possession of the spoils of victory – this battered hat and an excellent Christmas goose.

WATSON: Nice present for him. What did he do, then?

HOLMES: Well, being an honest fellow he wondered how to trace the owner. There was a card tied to the bird's leg with 'For Mrs. Henry Baker' printed on it.

[HOLMES *picks up the hat*]
On the lining of the hat here – look, you can just see it – there are the initials H. B.

WATSON: Henry Baker. But there must be hundreds of Henry Bakers in London.

HOLMES: Quite a few, certainly. Peterson hadn't a notion where to begin. That's why he brought the hat – and the goose – round to me on Christmas morning.

WATSON: Ah, I see.

HOLMES: We kept the goose until this morning. But it became, ah, obvious that in spite of the frost it needed eating without unnecessary delay. So I advised Peterson to carry it off to fulfil the ultimate destiny of a goose. Meanwhile, I retain the hat of the unknown gentleman who lost his Christmas dinner.

WATSON: He hasn't advertised, or anything?

HOLMES: No.

WATSON: You going to bother about him, then?

HOLMES: My dear Watson, you know how even the smallest problem interests me. There are certain clues. It's quite an eloquent old hat.

H

WATSON: Oh, the initials on the band. There's nothing else, surely?

[HOLMES *picks up the magnifying glass and hands it to him*]

HOLMES: You know my methods. Let's see what you can tell me about the owner of this hat.

[WATSON *takes the hat and proceeds to examine it, inside and out*]

WATSON [*thoughtfully*]: Mm! Mm! Well, there's no maker's name. . . .

HOLMES: A sound opening gambit, Watson.

WATSON: Mm! Silk lining – pretty discoloured, though.

HOLMES: Good!

WATSON: General condition of the hat, worse for wear. One or two cracks in it.

HOLMES: Excellent!

WATSON [*warming to the task*]: Lot of dust in the felt – and spots of something. Yes, and it looks as though he's being trying to cover some of the blemishes up with ink.

HOLMES: Capital, my dear Watson!

WATSON: Oh, the brim's been pierced for a hat-securer, but the elastic's missing. Otherwise, Holmes, it's just a very ordinary hat that's seen better days.

HOLMES: Then tell me what you deduce.

WATSON: Deduce?

HOLMES: Oh, Watson, you disappoint me. After such an admirable display of your powers of observation, too.

[WATSON *peers at the hat again*]

WATSON: Well, I don't know. No, I can't see anything.

HOLMES: You're too timid in drawing your inferences, that's your trouble. You've *seen* everything, but you haven't reasoned from what you've seen.

WATSON [*disappointed*] : Well, come on, Holmes – better tell me what I should've found.

[HOLMES *takes back the hat and fondles it as he speaks*]

HOLMES : This is the hat of a highly intellectual man who's also been well-to-do within the last three years, but has now fallen on hard times. He used to be a man of foresight, but he hasn't so much of it now. Moral retrogression, together with the decline of his fortunes. Drink, probably. Yes – that'd account for the fact that his wife has ceased to love him.

WATSON : My dear Holmes, what on earth are you talking about?

HOLMES [*ignoring the interruption*] : But he's retained some degree of self-respect. Middle-aged, grizzled hair. It's been cut within the last few days – and he likes to anoint it with lime cream.

WATSON [*amused sarcasm*] : Is that *all* you can find out?

HOLMES : Oh, and it's extremely probable that he hasn't the gas laid on in his house.

WATSON : Holmes, you're pulling my leg. Come on – own up, now!

HOLMES : Dear me, Watson, is it possible that even when I give you these results you still can't see how they're attained?

WATSON : No, I'm blessed if I can. How'd you know the man's an intellectual?

HOLMES : See what happens when I try the hat on?

[HOLMES *puts on the hat, which comes right down over his eyes*]

It comes right down over my eyes.

[*He removes the hat again*]

Cubic capacity, Watson. A man with a head large

enough to fit this hat must have something in all that brain.

WATSON [*laughs*]: I knew you were joking. What about the decline in his fortunes, then?

[HOLMES *points out the details, one by one*]

HOLMES: This hat is three years old. This is one of the first of these flat brims, curled at the edge.

WATSON: Ye-es.

HOLMES: You noticed the silk lining. It's a hat of the very best quality. If this man could afford to buy it three years ago, and he's still having to wear it in this state, then he's certainly gone down in the world.

WATSON: Granted, granted. But what about this 'foresight' and 'moral retrogression'?

HOLMES: Here – this hat securer. As you know, they're never on the hat when you buy it. So we gather that this man went out of his way to have one put in, as a precaution against the wind. But what's happened since? The elastic's got broken, and he's never had it replaced – *ergo*, he now has less foresight than before, and that's distinct proof of a weakening nature. But his self-respect hasn't gone entirely.

WATSON: No?

HOLMES: Well, look at the way he's tried to cover up some of the stains with ink. At least he's made some attempt.

WATSON: Yes, I'll have to give you that, too.

HOLMES: We can tell he's middle-aged, simply by examining the lining. See? All these greying hair-ends, cut off recently by the barber?

[WATSON *takes back the hat and sniffs at the lining, before returning it to* HOLMES]

WATSON: And the lime cream dressing – I can smell it!

HOLMES: As I told you. Now what else did I say?

WATSON [*amused*] : That his wife doesn't love him any more.

HOLMES : I'm afraid it's true. This hat hasn't been brushed for weeks.

WATSON : But he might be a bachelor!

HOLMES : Oh no. He was bringing home that goose as a peace-offering to his wife. Remember the card on its leg – to *Mrs. Henry Baker?*

WATSON : Holmes, you've an answer for everything. But how on earth can you tell from a man's hat that he hasn't the gas laid on in his house?

HOLMES : Quite simply. One tallow stain, or even two, might have got on to the hat by chance. But when I see no less than five, I begin to picture him walking upstairs at night with his hat in one hand and a candle in the other. Anyhow, he never got tallow stains on it from a gas jet. Satisfied?

WATSON [*laughing*] : Well, Holmes, it's all very ingenious. Remarkable! But there's been no crime committed. I mean, dash it, there's only the loss of a goose to consider. It all seems rather a waste of energy to me.

HOLMES : Watson, there are times when . . .

[*A knock at the door*]

Yes? Come in.

[*The door opens and* PETERSON *enters*]

PETERSON [*agitated*] : Mr. Holmes, sir. . . .

HOLMES : Peterson! What's the matter, man?

PETERSON : The goose! Mr. Holmes, Dr. Watson – the goose!

HOLMES : For heaven's sake, Peterson! Has it flown out of your kitchen window?

[PETERSON *holds out his hand to* HOLMES]

PETERSON : Look, sir. Look at this – what the missus found in its crop!

HOLMES: What . . .?

> [*He takes a large blue jewel from* PETERSON'S *palm and holds it up*]

WATSON: Great heavens!

HOLMES [*whistles*]

PETERSON: A diamond, Mr. Holmes, isn't it? I tried it on the window pane. It cut into the glass like putty.

WATSON: Precious stone, all right.

HOLMES: It's more than *a* precious stone.

PETERSON: What, sir?

HOLMES: It's *the* precious stone.

PETERSON: I – I don't catch how you mean, Mr. Holmes.

> [HOLMES *hands the jewel back to* PETERSON, *who gazes at it, awestruck*]

HOLMES: You should recognize it, Watson.

WATSON: Eh?

HOLMES: You must have seen the advertisement about it in the Agony Column every day lately.

WATSON: Not – you don't mean this is the Blue Carbuncle, Holmes? Countess of What's-her-name's?

HOLMES [*nodding*]: The Countess of Morcar's *Blue Carbuncle*. It's none other. I recognized its size and shape the moment I saw it. Any idea of the value you're holding in the palm of your hand, there, Peterson?

PETERSON: Well, I dunno. Quite a bit, eh? Hundred pounds, say?

HOLMES: I can see you don't appreciate such things. It's worth at least twenty times the amount they're offering as the finder's reward.

PETERSON: Reward, Mr. Holmes? How – how much?

HOLMES [simply]: A thousand pounds.

> [*A silence*]

PETERSON [*hoarsely*]: You – you wouldn't have me on, Mr. Holmes?

HOLMES: This is the stone, that's the reward, and you're the finder. Peterson, you're a rich man.

PETERSON: Cor! COR!

WATSON: Well, I'm blessed! *Where* did you say you found it?

PETERSON [*overwhelmed*]: It was in the goose, Dr. Watson – one Mr. Holmes said I was to take home and . . .

WATSON: Yes, yes, I've heard the whole story just now. But Holmes – wasn't the stone supposed to have been stolen from the Countess of Morcar's room at the Cosmopolitan?

HOLMES: Precisely.

WATSON: By a *goose*?

HOLMES [*laughing*]: Dear me, no. By one John Horner, a plumber. He'd been soldering a bar on to the grate in her room a few days before Christmas. He was left alone in the room for two or three minutes by Ryder, the head attendant.

PETERSON: Silly ass! Left the chap there, and when he came back the plumber had gone and the bureau had been forced.

WATSON: Ah, yes, I remember now. But they caught Horner, didn't they?

PETERSON: Same evening, sir. Didn't find the stone on him, though.

WATSON: That's right. There was something about him having a previous conviction for robbery, wasn't there?

PETERSON: Yes, sir. I reckon that clinched things against him. Remanded for the Assizes.

HOLMES: Well, the question for us to look into is the sequence

of events leading from a rifled jewel case at one end, to the crop of a goose in the Tottenham Court Road at the other.

WATSON: This Henry Baker, who lost the goose – do you think he's mixed up in it, Holmes?

HOLMES: Here is the stone. The stone came from the goose. The goose came from Mr. Henry Baker, the man with the bad hat and all the other characteristics *you* discovered, Watson.

WATSON: Thank you!

HOLMES: So now we must set ourselves to finding this gentleman. Hand me a slip of paper and that pencil, will you?

[WATSON *does so*]

Thank you. An advertisement must go into the evening papers.

[*Writing*]

'Found, at the corner of Goodge Street, a goose and a black felt hat. Mr. Henry Baker can have the same by applying at 6.30 this evening at 221B Baker Street.'

WATSON: Will he see it?

[HOLMES *hands the paper to* PETERSON]

HOLMES: Everyone who knows him will tell him about it. Peterson. . . .

PETERSON: Sir?

HOLMES: Be good enough to run down to the advertising agency and have this put in the evening papers, will you?

PETERSON: Which ones?

HOLMES: Oh, the *Globe, Star, Pall Mall, St. James's Gazette, Evening News, Standard, Echo* . . . Any others that occur to you.

PETERSON: Very good, Mr. Holmes. And the – er – stone, sir?

HOLMES: I'll keep that.

PETERSON: But . . .

HOLMES [*laughs*]: It's all right. Dr. Watson and I shan't abscond with your reward.

WATSON: You speak for yourself, Holmes!

> [*They all laugh.* PETERSON *hands the jewel back to* HOLMES]

HOLMES: Oh, and Peterson . . .

> [HOLMES *fishes in his waistcoat pocket, under the dressing-gown*]

PETERSON: Sir?

> [HOLMES *hands* PETERSON *a coin*]

HOLMES: Take this sovereign, for the advertisements. Use the change to buy a goose.

PETERSON: A goose, sir?

HOLMES: Bring it back here to me, will you? We must have one to give this gentleman in place of the one your family are preparing to devour.

PETERSON: Ah, I see! Very good, Mr. Holmes.

> [PETERSON *exits, closing the door*]

WATSON: Let's see that stone, Holmes.

> [HOLMES *hands it over,* WATSON *holds it to the light and squints at it*]

HOLMES: Yes – see how it glints and sparkles, Watson. Yet it's a nucleus and focus of crime. Every good stone is. They're the devil's pet baits.

WATSON: Mm!

HOLMES: There have been two murders, a vitriol-throwing, a suicide and several robberies, all over this forty-grain weight of crystallized charcoal. [*Sighs*] Who would think that so pretty a toy would be a purveyor to the gallows and the prison? Well, I'd better lock it in the strong-box

now and drop a line to the Countess, to let her know we have it.

WATSON [*handing it back*] : And I'd better get on with my professional rounds. Can't stay here gossiping all day, you know.

HOLMES [*amused*] : No, Watson. Of course not.

WATSON: Er – I'll be back this evening, though. Like to see if there are any answers to that advertisement.

HOLMES: Very good, my dear fellow. I dine at seven. There's a woodcock, I believe. In view of recent occurrences, though, perhaps I'd better ask Mrs. Hudson to examine its crop.

> [*They laugh as* WATSON *exits, leaving* HOLMES *standing looking at the jewel. Blackout, or curtain fall, to denote passage of time*]

> [*The scene as before.* HOLMES *has now discarded the dressing-gown in favour of a jacket. A goose lies prominently on the sideboard.* HENRY BAKER, *dressed for the street, stands facing* HOLMES. *They are examining the hat. There is a knock at the door and* WATSON *enters in street clothes*]

HOLMES: Ah, Watson, come in. This is my colleague and friend, Dr. Watson. Watson, this is Mr. Henry Baker. You only just missed him on the stair.

> [WATSON *and* BAKER *shake hands*]

WATSON: ⎫
BAKER: ⎭ How d'ye do, sir?

> [WATSON *throws his coat and hat aside*]

WATSON: Sorry I'm late, Holmes. Delayed on a case.

HOLMES: Quite all right. Now, Mr. Baker – is this your hat?

BAKER: Yes, sir, that is undoubtedly my hat, and I'm sorry you've been troubled, sir. To tell the truth, shillings

haven't been so plentiful with me as they once were. I'd no doubt that the ruffians who assaulted me had carried off both my hat and the bird, and I didn't care to spend more money with little hope of recovering them.

HOLMES: Very naturally. [*Casually*] Oh, by the way, about the bird – we were compelled to eat it.

BAKER: Eat it!

HOLMES: It would have been no use to anyone if we had not done so, I can assure you. [*Watching for reaction*] But I presume that this other goose on the sideboard will answer your purpose equally well?

> [*He indicates the goose.* BAKER *gives it a prod with his finger*]

BAKER [*pleased*]: Certainly, certainly! It's very civil of you, sir.

HOLMES [*still watching him closely*]: We still have the feathers, legs – crop – and so on of your own bird about the place.

BAKER [*laughs*]: Well, sir, they might be useful relics of my adventure, but I can hardly see what other use they are going to be.

HOLMES [*satisfied*]: Very true. Then here's your hat, Mr. Baker.

> [HOLMES *hands* BAKER *the hat.* WATSON *lifts the goose and gives it to him*]

WATSON: And here's your bird.

BAKER: Very fine, too.

HOLMES: Oh, by the way – would it bore you to tell me where you got that other goose from? I'm something of a fowl-fancier, and I've seldom seen a better-grown goose.

BAKER: Not at all. A few of us frequent the Alpha Inn near the British Museum. Do you know it?

WATSON: Yes, I do.

BAKER: This year our good host, Windigate, got up a goose

club. We put in a few pence a week and each of us was to have a bird for Christmas. Nice bird, as you say.

HOLMES: Very tasty! I hope this other will be adequate compensation.

[BAKER *slings the goose over his shoulder*]

BAKER: It's only a pity you didn't take a fancy to this old bonnet of mine as well. Scarcely fitted to my years or my dignity any longer. Well, goodnight to you, gentlemen. . . .

[*He turns to go*]

WATSON: Mr. Baker. . . .

[BAKER *turns back.* HOLMES *looks surprised*]

BAKER: Yes, sir?

WATSON: Er – have you by any chance the gas laid on at your home?

BAKER: The gas?

[HOLMES *stifles amusement*]

WATSON [*embarrassed*]: I – er – I'm considering installing it myself. Er – I wondered – your opinion, you know.

BAKER [*sadly*]: A splendid facility, I understand, Doctor. Alas – the expense, you know.

WATSON: Oh, quite, quite! Outrageous!

[BAKER *puts his hat on the back of his head and moves to the door*]

BAKER: Then, good night, and the compliments of the season to you.

WATSON: Compliments of the season.

[BAKER *exits.* HOLMES *explodes with mirth.* WATSON *joins in*]

HOLMES: Really, Watson! I wonder you didn't ask him about his wife, too!

WATSON: I might have known you'd be right, Holmes.

HOLMES: Of course. At any rate, it's quite certain he knows nothing of this matter. Now, you're not particularly hungry, are you?

WATSON [*he is*]: Well, I. . . .

HOLMES: Good. I suggest we ask Mrs. Hudson to preserve our woodcock for supper. We must follow up this clue while it's hot.

> [WATSON *gives a resigned sigh. They begin to move towards the door,* WATSON *picking up his coat and hat. Curtain as they prepare to leave*]

SCENE TWO

[Interior of the Alpha Inn. A bar counter at left, behind which MR. WINDIGATE is serving. Several men are standing about, drinking and talking together, and men and women are sitting at a table drinking. Ad lib conversation and laughter. WINDIGATE is taking a customer's money as HOLMES and WATSON enter, right, both wearing street clothes. They approach the bar as the customer moves away]

WINDIGATE: Good evening, gen'lemen.

HOLMES:
WATSON: } Good evening, landlord.

WINDIGATE: And what may your pleasure be this evening?

WATSON: Holmes?

HOLMES: Beer. Two pints of beer, please.

WINDIGATE: And a better drop you won't find north of the river, sir.

[He proceeds to draw two pints]

HOLMES: It should be excellent if it's as good as your geese, Mr. Windigate.

WINDIGATE: Geese, sir? *My* geese?

HOLMES: I was speaking only half an hour ago to a member of your goose-club – Mr. Henry Baker.

WINDIGATE: Ah, yes, I follow you! But them's not *our* geese, of course.

WATSON: Oh? Whose, then?

WINDIGATE: I got the whole two dozen from a chap in Covent Garden.

[*He serves the beer.* WATSON *pays*]

HOLMES: Indeed?

WINDIGATE: Breckinridge is his name. You know him, sir?

HOLMES: Breckinridge? No. But no matter.

[*He picks up his glass.* WATSON *follows suit*]

Here's your good health, landlord, and prosperity to your house.

WATSON: Good health!

WINDIGATE: And the compliments of the season to you, gentlemen!

[HOLMES *and* WATSON *drink. Black out*]

SCENE THREE

[*In Covent Garden market. A poultry barrow at right with the name 'Breckinridge' painted on it. It is lit by lanterns and bears a few turkeys and chickens for sale – but NO geese. A few people move to and fro, huddled up against the cold.* BRECKINRIDGE *and* BILL *stand beside the stall, flapping their arms to keep warm.* HOLMES *and* WATSON *enter from left, their coat collars turned up against the wind.* BRECKINRIDGE *picks up a chicken and dangles it under the nose of a passing woman*]

BRECKINRIDGE: Now, missis – what about a treat for the old man?

[*The woman ignores him. He makes a derisory gesture after her and throws the bird back on the stall in disgust.* BILL *opens a newspaper and leans against the stall*]

HOLMES [*approaching*]: Good evening. Cold again.

BRECKINRIDGE: Perishin'.

HOLMES: Oh! Sold out of geese?

BRECKINRIDGE: Let you have five hundred tomorrow, guv.

HOLMES: I'd sooner have one just now.

[BRECKINRIDGE *jerks his thumb towards off-stage right*]

BRECKINRIDGE: Try 'im over there – with the gas flare. He's got some left.

HOLMES: Oh dear – I was specially recommended to you.

BRECKINRIDGE: Recommended?

HOLMES: By the landlord of the Alpha – up by the Museum.

BRECKINRIDGE: Oh, 'sright. Sent him a couple o'dozen.

HOLMES: Very fine birds, too.

WATSON: Beautiful.

HOLMES: Where do you manage to get such specimens?

BRECKINRIDGE [*becoming suspicious*]: Now then, mister – what you drivin' at?

HOLMES: I beg your pardon?

BRECKINRIDGE: Let's 'ave it straight out, now!

HOLMES: I simply wondered who sold you the geese you supplied to the Alpha.

BRECKINRIDGE: All right, then – I'm not telling. You'd think they was the only perishin' geese left in the world. First this other chap pestering me, and now you!

WATSON: Other chap? What. . . .

HOLMES [*not letting Watson continue*]: I've no connexion with anyone else's inquiries, I can assure you. If you won't tell me, then the bet's off, that's all.

BRECKINRIDGE: Bet? What bet?

HOLMES: I like to think I know a fowl's quality. I'm ready to back my opinion on it. Half a dozen mouthfuls of one of those geese last night and I put a fiver on it that I was eating a country-bred bird.

BRECKINRIDGE: Oh, you did, eh? Well, I'll tell you this much – you've lost your fiver.

HOLMES: Town-bred! I don't believe it.

BRECKINRIDGE: Listen, I've been handlin' fowls since I was a nipper. I tell you every one of them birds that went to the Alpha was town-bred.

HOLMES [*laughs*]: You'll never persuade me to believe that. I'd take another bet on it – with you, if you like.

BRECKINRIDGE [*passionately*]: All right! All right!

[*He turns to* BILL]

I

Bill!

[BILL *hastily emerges from the newspaper*]

BILL: Guv'nor?

BRECKINRIDGE: Bring us the books out 'ere — and look slippy!

BILL: Yes, guv.

[BILL *goes round the back of the barrow*]

BRECKINRIDGE: Now then, Mr. Cocksure, you just wait a minute and we'll see. A sovereign, was it, you said?

HOLMES: If you're sure you can afford it.

BRECKINRIDGE: Won't be me havin' to afford it, mate. [*Shouts*] Where are yer with them books?

[BILL *hurries back, carrying some ledgers*]

BILL: 'ere y'are, guv'nor.

BRECKINGRIDGE: Ta.

[*He takes the ledgers.* BILL *returns to his newspaper*]

BRECKINRIDGE: See this book?

HOLMES: I do.

[BRECKINRIDGE *opens a ledger and turns pages*]

BRECKINRIDGE: This is the list of folk I buy from. Now — page fifty-seven — bit farther — fifty-eight, fifty-nine, sixty! Now, then, what's the last entry you see?

[*He thrusts the ledger under* WATSON'S *nose*]

WATSON: Er — let me see. [*Reads*] 'Mrs. Oakshott, 117 Brixton Road, December 22nd. . . . Twenty-four geese at seven and six.'

BRECKINRIDGE [*triumphantly*]: Brixton Road. Town or country?

WATSON: Town, of course.

BRECKINRIDGE: Much obliged. Now what's it say underneath?

WATSON [*peering*]: Er – [*Reads*] 'Sold to Mr. Windigate, at the Alpha – twelve shillings each.'

BRECKINRIDGE: And that'll cost you just one sovereign – and cheap at the price.

HOLMES [*annoyed*]: Ridiculous! I'd never have believed it.

[*He fishes out a coin*]

Here you are, my man.

[*He gives* BRECKINRIDGE *the coin grudgingly*]

Good evening to you.

[HOLMES *turns curtly away left, followed by* WATSON]

BRECKINRIDGE [*calling after them, with a derisory gesture*]: And the compliments of the season to *you*!

[HOLMES *and* WATSON *wander away to extreme left, while the crowd surges to and fro.* BRECKIN- RIDGE *holds up a chicken, but there are no takers. The crowd recedes*]

WATSON: Well, Holmes?

[HOLMES *begins to chuckle and then laugh, joined by* WATSON]

HOLMES: Cheap at the price, as our friend observed.

WATSON: Lucky for you he was a betting man.

HOLMES: My dear Watson, when you see a man with whiskers of that cut and the *Pink 'Un* sticking out of his pocket you can always draw him with a bet.

[RYDER *enters right and approaches* BRECKIN- RIDGE *who does not see him immediately.* BRECKINRIDGE *suddenly notices* RYDER *with displeasure. A dumb-show argument starts between them*]

WATSON: Hear what he said about being pestered, Holmes? Sounds as though we aren't the only ones interested in what became of those geese.

HOLMES: I did indeed.

> [HOLMES *and* WATSON *notice the argument going on*]

Listen to that, Watson!

BRECKINRIDGE [*loudly*]: And I tell you I've had enough of you and your perishin' geese. If you come asking questions again I'll set the dog on you – straight I will.

RYDER: But I tell you one of them belonged to me. She told me to ask you.

BRECKINRIDGE: You can go and ask the King of Proosher for all I care. Go on! Get out of here!

> [*He makes a threatening gesture.* RYDER *moves away towards* HOLMES *and* WATSON]

RYDER [*over his shoulder*]: All right, all right – I'm going!

WATSON: Watson, this may save us a visit to the Brixton Road. Come on!

> [HOLMES *and* WATSON *move in to intercept* RYDER *as he is about to exit left.* BRECKIN-RIDGE, *like* BILL, *vanishes behind a newspaper*]

HOLMES: Just a moment, my good man!

RYDER: Yes? What is it?

HOLMES: My friend and I couldn't help overhearing your little argument just now. I think we could be of assistance to you.

RYDER [*suspiciously*]: You? What do you know about it?

HOLMES: I make it my business to know what other people don't know.

RYDER [*preparing to move on*]: Well, you don't know anything about this.

HOLMES [*detaining him*]: Excuse me, I know everything about it. You are endeavouring to trace some geese which were sold by Mrs. Oakshott, of Brixton Road, to that stall-

holder there. He sold them to Mr. Windigate, of the Alpha Inn.

RYDER [*eagerly*]: Then – you know where some of them went?

HOLMES: I do.

RYDER: Then you're just the man I've been wanting to meet. I'll make it worth your while.

HOLMES: I'm sure you will. But may we know whom we have the pleasure of assisting?

RYDER [*hesitantly*]: My name is John Robinson.

HOLMES: No, the *real* name, if you please.

RYDER [*reluctantly*]: Well . . . my name is James Ryder.

HOLMES: Head attendant at the Cosmopolitan Hotel, if I'm not mistaken. Watson, get a cab, will you?

WATSON: Right. Hey, cabby! Cabby! Over here!

[*He hurries off left, waving his stick*]

HOLMES: I think a cosy room would be better than this windswept market place. I'm sure I shall be able to tell you everything you wish to know.

[*Black out. If desired, we could hear effects of a hansom cab coming to a halt, its door slamming, and the cab moving off, while the props are being removed*]

SCENE FOUR

[221B *Baker Street, as before. The curtains are drawn and the lamp on the table lit with a low flame.* HOLMES *enters, followed by* RYDER *and* WATSON, *who closes the door.* HOLMES *and* WATSON *throw aside their street clothes,* RYDER *keeping his on, fiddling nervously with his cap*]

HOLMES: Pray take the basket chair, Ryder.

RYDER: Thank you, sir.

[*He sits.* HOLMES *pushes the lamp closer to* RYDER *and turns up the flame, so that the light falls mostly on* RYDER's *face.* HOLMES *draws up a chair opposite him, and* WATSON *stands behind it in the shadows*]

HOLMES: Now, you want to know what became of those geese?

RYDER: That's right.

HOLMES: Or rather, I fancy, of *that goose* – white, with a black bar across the tail, if I remember correctly.

RYDER [*excited*]: You remember that one!

HOLMES: Oh, distinctly. As a matter of fact, it came here.

RYDER: Here!

HOLMES: Yes, and a most remarkable bird it proved to be. I don't wonder that you should take an interest in it. It laid an egg after it was dead – the bonniest, brightest little blue egg that ever was seen.

RYDER [*cringing back*]: Who – who are you?

HOLMES: My name is Sherlock Holmes.

RYDER: Sherlock Holmes!

HOLMES: The game's up, Ryder, and you know it.

[RYDER *groans and buries his face in his hands*]

Think we could spare a drop of brandy, Watson?

WATSON: Looks as though we'd better.

[*He goes to the sideboard and pours a glass of brandy from a decanter, then pauses*]

Holmes?

HOLMES: It's a cold night, Watson – why not?

[WATSON *smiles and pours two more glasses. He gives* HOLMES *one, then nudges* RYDER, *who accepts the glass almost automatically and gulps the brandy down.* HOLMES *and* WATSON *raise their glasses silently to one another and take a sip*]

There, Watson! He looks a little more human now.

RYDER [*subdued*]: I'm all right, sir.

HOLMES: Capital! Well, we already have nearly all the proof we need, but we may as well have everything complete.

RYDER: It was Catherine Cusack told me about that stone, sir.

HOLMES: The Countess of Morcar's waiting-maid?

RYDER: That's her.

HOLMES: I see. And the temptation of sudden wealth was too much for you.

RYDER: I'm not the first.

HOLMES: It seems to me, Ryder, that you've the makings of a very pretty villain in you. You knew this man Horner, the plumber, had been in trouble before. You and your friend Cusack invented some small job in her ladyship's room and managed that Horner should be the man sent for to attend to it. As soon as he'd left you rifled the jewel-case, raised the alarm and had the unfortunate man arrested.

RYDER [*earnestly*] : Mr. Holmes, sir, it was just like you say. Sir, I never went wrong before – never. I never will again – I swear it to you. [*To* WATSON] And to you, sir.

[WATSON *draws himself up severely*]

WATSON: Hm!

[RYDER *slips forward on to his knees before* HOLMES]

RYDER: I beg you, sir – don't bring it into court. My father and mother, sir – I'd do anything rather than . . .

HOLMES [*interrupting*] : We'll talk about that later. Meanwhile, sit down again and let us have a true account of what occurred *after* the robbery.

WATSON: Yes; how did the stone get into that goose? And how did the goose come into the open market?

[RYDER *resumes his seat*]

RYDER: I'll tell you everything. When Horner had been arrested it seemed best for me to get straight away with the stone before the police took it into their heads to search all the hotel staff. I made for my sister's place. She's married to a chap named Oakshott, in the Brixton Road.

WATSON: I see!

RYDER: All the way, every man I met seemed to be a policeman or looked like a detective. I was in a cold sweat before I got there. My sister asked why I was so pale. I said I'd take a breath of fresh air, and I went out into the yard to smoke a pipe.

HOLMES: And?

RYDER: While I was wondering what to do I suddenly realized there was geese waddling all round me. And I got the idea to beat the best detective that ever lived. My sister had told me I might have the pick of the flock

for a Christmas present. Well, it was obvious – I'd take the goose there and then, get it to swallow the jewel, and it wouldn't matter who searched my room between then and Christmas dinner-time: they'd never think of looking inside a goose.

WATSON: Very ingenious indeed. And that was what you did, then?

RYDER: Yes, sir. I caught a fine big bird, and it swallowed the stone without any trouble at all when I put it in its bill. But it flapped and struggled like anything till I let it go, so I had to go in and fetch my sister and ask her to help me catch the goose with the black bar across its tail for my Christmas present. Well, we caught it, and she killed it, and I carried it home. As soon as I got home I took a knife and opened it up. There wasn't a sign of the stone.

HOLMES: So we gather.

WATSON: What did you do, then?

RYDER: Do? I was back to my sister's as fast as I could go to ask if there was another goose with a black bar across the tail.

HOLMES: And, of course, there was.

RYDER: It was twins with mine. They couldn't tell 'em apart. Only, by the time I got there the second one had gone. That fellow Breckinridge had called at my sister's and bought the whole blessed lot!

WATSON [*laughs heartily*].

RYDER [*bitterly*]: Oh, you can laugh, sir! I went to Breckinridge's stall that afternoon, but he wasn't telling me anything, and then I tried again tonight, when you saw me. [*Beginning to break down*] It's just my luck, all of it. I might have known it all along. I've been honest all my life, gentlemen, and now, here I am, branded as

a thief and I've hardly even set eyes on the thing I stole.

[HOLMES *rises and points to the door*]

HOLMES: Get out, Ryder!

RYDER: Sir?

HOLMES: I said get out!

[RYDER *gets up and begins backing towards the door*]

RYDER: Oh, yes, Mr. Holmes. Heaven bless you, sir! It'll never happen again, as long as I live.

[RYDER *turns and scurries out*]

WATSON [*laughs*]: Well, well, Holmes – so you're letting him go free.

HOLMES: If Horner were in danger, that would be another thing. But Ryder will never be able to appear as a witness against him now. The case is finished.

WATSON: And the countess will get her Blue Carbuncle back.

HOLMES: She'll never miss the reward she'll have to pay to Peterson, and it'll make all the difference to him. So everyone profits, in some way.

[HOLMES *moves into the chair previously occupied by* RYDER, *so that the light falls sharply upon his face.* WATSON *takes* HOLMES'S *seat*]

You know, I think it's just possible that I've saved his soul. He'll never yield to temptation again, and a stretch in gaol would probably have turned him into a gaolbird for life. He has cause to be grateful. Besides, it's the season of forgiveness.

WATSON: Yes, Holmes. Quite right!

HOLMES: As for you and me, chance has put in our way a most singular and whimsical problem, and its solution is its reward. And now, if you'll have the goodness to touch

that bell, my dear Watson, we will begin another investigation – in which also a bird will be the chief feature.

> [WATSON *reaches out to press the bell, which rings in the distance.* HOLMES *and* WATSON *silently raise their glasses to one another and drink as the curtain falls*]

All the Sherlock Holmes stories are contained in the two Omnibus volumes.

THE COMPLETE SHERLOCK HOLMES SHORT STORIES

THE COMPLETE SHERLOCK HOLMES LONG STORIES

and also in the Uniform Edition

Adventures of Sherlock Holmes

Case-book of Sherlock Holmes

Memoirs of Sherlock Holmes

Return of Sherlock Holmes

Hound of the Baskervilles

Valley of Fear

Sign of Four

His Last Bow

Full details of the above titles, and all the works of Sir Arthur Conan Doyle can be obtained on request from the address below.

JOHN MURRAY

50 Albemarle Street London WI

Sherlock Holmes Investigates

Stories by Sir Arthur Conan Doyle
selected and introduced by

MICHAEL and MOLLIE HARDWICK

'Michael and Mollie Hardwick have prefaced six of the most popular Holmes cases by setting the scene of the London of the time and recalling the first meeting of Holmes and Watson for readers making the acquaintance of the famous pair for the first time. They have made an excellent informative job of it.'

Manchester Evening Chronicle

'A volume for new readers with Paget illustrations. Holmes has the marvellous gift of discovering a world and Conan Doyle's achievement has been to bring Poe to the Home Counties and there are no more delightful moments in this selection of stories than the long drives out of gaslight into Surrey or Kent, with Holmes now whipping up the horse, now driving with his head sunk deep on his breast.'

The New Statesman

Sidney Paget illustrations

The Man who was Sherlock Holmes

MICHAEL and MOLLIE HARDWICK

'Many glimpses of the evolution of Holmes . . . they succeed in producing a portrait of a writer who fits into no obvious pattern. Those coming fresh to the Master will find it fascinating.'

The Evening Standard

'Bluff, hale Dr Doyle never seemed in his lifetime very close to the austere detective he invented but here the similarities are picked out —the scientific training, the artistic family background, the persistence, imagination, courage and sensitivity. And of course Doyle did apply Holmes' methods of deduction.'

The Daily Telegraph

The Sherlock Holmes Companion

MICHAEL and MOLLIE HARDWICK

'The Sherlock Holmes Companion is authentic: has the atmosphere of Baker Street, is well docketed. There are excellent illustrations and a section with captivating plot summaries that invite re-reading. A valuable handbook.'

The Daily Telegraph

'Every student of the sacred writing will want not only to read but to possess The Sherlock Holmes Companion and . . . the incomparable evocative drawings Sidney Paget made.'

The Birmingham Post

'There is much in this scholarly work of reference to delight students of the Baker Street saga.'

The Southern Echo

'Much of the book is taken up by a complete Who's Who of all the named characters in the stories, followed by a brief analysis of plots and dates. The compilers then provide an engaging sampler of quotations from Holmes and Watson . . . This pleasantly produced book contains a treasure more valuable than any commentator's words, however, it is studded with drawings by Sidney Paget.'

Times Literary Supplement

'A *must* for all addicts.' *Evening News*

'Attractive, hand-sized, well thought-out, well-written, very accurate and entertaining.' *Sherlock Holmes Journal*

60 Sidney Paget drawings

The Exploits of Sherlock Holmes

ADRIAN CONAN DOYLE

and JOHN DICKSON CARR

'For the lover of Holmes, there can be no question about this book; it is excellent in every way. Here are twelve stories all written about cases actually referred to in the original Holmes books, all well-written, and, to the non-expert eye, all most successful in recapturing the authentic Baker Street atmosphere.'   *The Birmingham Post*

'How do the new stories compare with the originals? They are in the true canon. A book which is certain to give an enormous amount of pleasure to all interested in the Holmes saga.'   *Glasgow Herald*

The Life of Sir Arthur Conan Doyle

JOHN DICKSON CARR

'Let me say at once it is worth every farthing of its cost. Mr Dickson Carr has written a fine, bustling book with enough sheer stingo in it to fill a dozen thrillers. It is full of fascinating new facts and fresh stories.'
The News Chronicle

'The adventure of an eager, chivalrous and courageous nature, accepting life in all its manifestations with enormous gusto.'   *The Sunday Times*

3rd printing Illustrated